BUILD IT

EMPLOYEE

HOW TO GET YOUR EMPLOYEES

SHARE

TO THINK AND ACT

OWNERSHIP

LIKE BUSINESS OWNERS

PLANS

. . . .

Craig West

Craig West
Succession Plus Pty Ltd
Level 3, 50 York St
Sydney NSW 2000
www.successionplus.com.au

Published by:
Boolarong Press
38/1631 Wynnum Road
Tingalpa Qld 4173
Australia.
www.boolarongpress.com.au

First published 2019

A catalogue record for this book is available from the National Library of Australia

ISBN: 9781925877106

Editor: Amelia Stuckey, Words Unstuck

Typeset in Museo Sans 10 pt by Boolarong Press

Printed and bound in China by Everbest Printing Investment Limited

Disclaimer

The material in this publication is of the nature of general comment only, and neither purports nor intends to be advice. Readers should not act on the basis of any matter in this publication without considering (and if appropriate, taking) professional advice with due regard to their own particular circumstances. The author and publisher expressly disclaim all and any liability to any person, whether a purchaser of this publication or not, in respect of anything and of the consequences of anything done or omitted to be done by any such person in reliance, whether whole or partial, upon the whole or any part of the contents of this publication.

CONTENTS

INTRODUCTION

I've been a strategic accountant and adviser to small businesses for more than 20 years – and throughout that time I have identified a number of key steps that business owners can take to dramatically improve the financial performance of their businesses. One of these is having an employee incentive program that motivates staff to think and act less like employees and more like business owners. The ability to attract, retain and motivate people to peak performance means being able to attract and retain business – and it is a significant competitive advantage. In fact, it can mean the difference between success and failure.

Until now the most attractive employee incentive systems have been created to meet the needs of large corporates rather than smaller companies. In this book we highlight the Peak Performance Trust (PPT), an employee equity plan that has been created specifically to give smaller companies access to the same sophisticated incentive benefits that are used by large companies. The PPT enables you to create a structure within which your employees' lifestyle and financial goals are aligned with your business objectives. The result? A cohesive and committed team that is single-minded about working toward, and sharing in, the benefits of a successful and profitable business.

This book is broken up into 3 parts:

- Part 1 – gives you an overview of the key issues involved in implementing a Peak Performance Trust (PPT) within your company. It is a general discussion for business owners who want an overview of ESOPs and in particular PPTs
- Part 2 – provides more technical explanation for accountants, financial planners and business owners on how ESOPs work
- Part 3 – provides the academic research behind how and why ESOPs exist and the use of ESOPs as a viable business succession and exit planning tool.

When you're ready to talk about how a PPT can benefit your company's growth and profitability, you'll have a good understanding of the requirements and scope of the process. So please, enjoy this short read and then let's talk about your peak performance needs.

Craig West
Managing Director and Founder
Succession Plus

PS. For more worksheets, articles, advice and information on employee incentive schemes visit www.successionplus.com.au.
1300 665 473 | cwest@successionplus.com.au

SUCCESSION

• PART 1

OVERVIEW OF ESOPs

Is this the competitive edge you've been overlooking?

"People are definitely a company's greatest asset.
It doesn't make any difference whether the product
is cars or cosmetics. A company is only as good
as the people it keeps."

Mary Kay Ash

Staff recruitment, satisfaction, motivation and retention are often dismissed as being part of the 'soft' skill set – of lesser importance than the real business of generating revenues and earning profits. But ask any owner of a small or medium-sized business what his or her greatest challenge yet most valuable asset is, and all will agree – it's their staff. What would it mean to your business if your employees were as committed to achieving success as you are? Recent surveys confirm what most owners of small and medium-sized businesses know only too well – their number one concern, above even cash flow problems or a lack of sales, is finding and keeping the best people. In an employment market that is experiencing the impacts of an ageing workforce, skills shortages and a new generation of employees that is more mobile, more demanding and less loyal to employers, employee retention is becoming one of today's hottest competitive issues.

Not investing in your employees is too expensive

Employee turnover can represent significant costs to businesses in terms of:
- recruitment and training
- disruption to the team dynamic
- disruption to relationships with customers, suppliers and other third parties
- disruption to business continuity
- and a variety of other direct and indirect costs.

One estimate suggests that businesses lose at least two months of productive time through recruitment, training, loss of momentum and other factors when a staff member leaves. And it is said to cost anywhere from two and a half to three times a person's annual salary before the business is up to speed again – not to mention the cost of the intellectual property and business knowledge that has just walked out the door. Simply, losing staff means replacement costs, foregone opportunities and even increased competition if that's whose recruiting your best performers. According to the PWC Family Business Survey in 2014,

48% of SMEs said that their biggest internal business issue was staff recruitment, followed by business and product development as well as cash flow and cost control challenges.

Employee incentive schemes as a strategic business tool

Recruiting staff is an expensive, time consuming and often haphazard process. And in a job market where the best candidates are often interviewing you, rather than the other way around, businesses need to find ways of differentiating themselves through innovative and attractive terms of employment.

Specific strategies aimed at attracting, motivating and retaining employees can deliver valuable payoffs. Employee incentive schemes that get your people thinking and acting less like employees and more like business owners are an important tool. Their primary objective (and the reason for their success) is to align your employees' financial objectives with those of your business – and that translates into a major competitive advantage.

Research shows that Employee Share Ownership Plans (ESOPs) are identified as a means of enhancing enterprise performance through promoting worker productivity. (Relations., 2000) There have also been studies related to use as a means of reducing agency costs through directly monitoring employees and through adopting incentive-based forms of remuneration. (Pendleton, 2006)

A Principal – agent behavioural theory argues that employee logical self-interest, aversion to risk and effort creates costs for an organisation. In the absence of complete information, the principal (business owner) has to increase productivity through a mixture of compensation and monitoring of agents (employees). ESOPs are a way to align principal and agents efforts to improve productivity, however, a free rider effect is expected to diminish the effect of ESOPs in larger firms. (Sesil & Lin, 2011)

They have also been argued to reduce wealth inequality and improve firm and aggregate economic outcomes (Kozlowski, 2013). ESOPs are also considered by policy makers and advocates to be an important mechanism to encourage Start-up activity by enabling Australian employers to improve cash flows and attract and retain talented staff at lower rates of wage compensation (when supplemented with shares or options) (Department of Prime Minister and Cabinet, 2014).

This is all evident in Computershare's Employee Share Plan Survey in 2017, which found:

- 52% of plan participants say that the plan reduced the chance they would leave the company either "to a great extent" or "to some extent"
- 63% of participants feel "very loyal" to the company, and
- 73% of plan participants agree or strongly agree that the company is a good place to work.

Why do workers get into an ESOP?

In a recent Melbourne University study, a group of employees were asked certain questions and below are what they ranked as the most important elements of an ESOP:

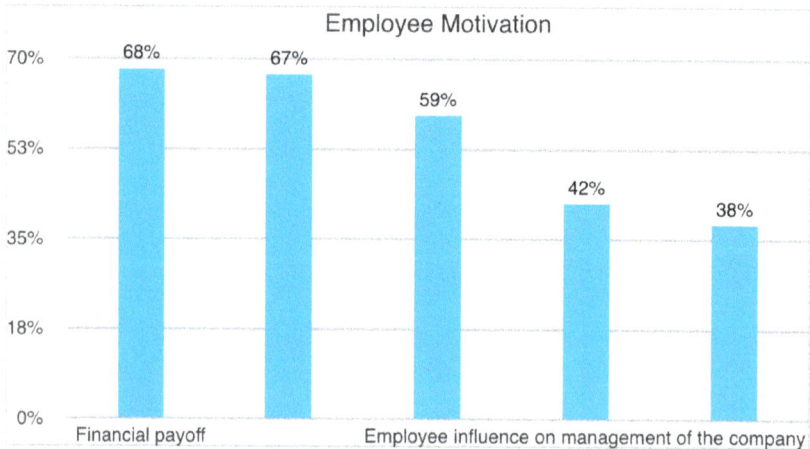

Source: Michelle Brown, Rowan Minson, Ann O'Connell and Ian Ramsay, Why Do Employees Participate in Employee Share Ownership Plans? Employee Share Ownership Project, Melbourne Law School, The University of Melbourne, 2011.

ESOPS are used for several reasons:

- **Savings Vehicle** – Most ESOP plans have a long-term focus (3-7 years), allowing employees to accumulate savings through acquiring and holding shares.
- **Participation** – ESOP participants tend to experience a greater sense of community and involvement with the decision-making process, leading to increases in employee engagement levels.
- **Succession Planning** – An ESOP can be an effective employee buy-out instrument when the owner(s) want to retire (or change their business direction) and need to sell. Funding Retirement – ESOPs can give founders the ability to extract cash prior to retirement.

Case Studies

Below are examples of businesses in Australia that have introduced ESOPs into their business:

LJ Hooker Commercial real estate office on the Central Coast was the Winner of the 2011 ESOP of the Year award using a Peak Performance Trust. The award was based on substantial reduction in sick days and improved staff retention, as well as a noted increase in performance and participation.

Ty Blanche of LJ Hooker said "we have created a more understanding team of people, and added value to the individual's performance congruently."

"Both financial services and property management referrals from employees participating in this scheme increased at a higher level than before. I put this down to their seeing value in contributing to the company's bottom line because they will share in the profit."

The National Personnel Group said "since kicking off our Ownership Thinking program, absenteeism has already dropped by at least one third! Overall, productivity is higher and our employees are taking more interest in the financial wellbeing of the business."

Academic Research on the Impact of ESOPs

- ESOPs appear to increase sales, employment and sales per employee (Drs. Joseph R. Blasi and Doulas L. Kruse School of Management and Labor Relations Rutgers University).
- ESOP companies that combine employee ownership with a participative management style grow 8-11% per year faster than they otherwise would have been expected to grow based on pre-ESOP performance (National Center for Employee Ownership, Harvard Business Review September/October 1987).
- Compared to 500 private non-ESOP companies, ESOP companies paid better benefits, had twice the retirement income for employees, and paid higher wages than their non-ESOP counterparts. (Wealth and Income Consequences of Employee Ownership: A Comparative Study from Washington State, Kardas, Peter A., Scharft, Adria L., Keogh, Jim, November 1998).
- Studies between ESOPs and productivity growth have found greater productivity and profitability in the first few years after a company adopts an ESOP (Dr Doulas L. Kruse, School of Management and Labor Relations, Rutgers University, 1995).
- The number of ESOPs in the UK increased by 10% during 2012 (National Centre for Employee Ownership, February 2013).

While the research undoubtedly shows an increase in employees looking for equity in the business they work for – Australia lags behind on the world stage in providing a mechanism to achieve this. According to recent research in both the United States and Europe, a little over 30% of employees have some kind of equity interest in the business they work for, while in Australia that number is around 8%. Of the estimated $8 trillion of corporate equity in the United States, employees own about $213 billion through ESOPs and similar stock plans.

One of the main reasons for this low participation rate is that many businesses don't realise that share ownership is appropriate for them, even though it can be used in any business – even those that are not publicly listed on an exchange. Equity replicator plans can replicate the operations of share plans without the need for shares. These plans create units, which represent notional equity, and awards are calculated by using a formula that measures business value.

ESOPs and Gen Y

A workshop on generation Y in the workplace raised an interesting statistic; 72% of the Generation Y population want to own their own business. Back in my dad's generation less than 12% of school leavers wanted to run their own business. Most people wanted to go and work for a big bank or a corporate and stay there till they were 65 then retire on a good retirement plan.

If you have Generation Y employees this is an important point to know, as they may leave to pursue their goals if equity ownership is not an option. However, another interesting statistic was that over 90% of those wanting to own a business said they didn't want to own it on their own. Generation Y workers look for freedom and flexibility and the opportunity to have three months off to travel to Europe.

Most baby boomers look at that and think it's all too hard, they get it too easy or they are too much risk. But the fact is this is the way our workforce is heading, and rather than fight it we need to look for ways to accommodate it so that we can retain good people.

Most 25-year-olds can't afford to start their own business or buy one. So, an employee share plan gives younger employees the opportunity to part own a business while enjoying the security and lifestyle that comes with being an employee. And over the next five to ten years, that employee has an opportunity to build equity and gradually take over ownership of the business, if they want it.

A strategic approach to remuneration

"Research indicates that workers have three
prime needs: interesting work, recognition
for doing a good job, and being let in
on things that are going on in the company."

Zig Ziglar

Far from just paying people a standard wage or salary and providing the minimum mandatory benefits (such as company-funded superannuation and basic leave entitlements), your remuneration strategy should help you to attract the best people, to get the best performance from them once they're on the job, and encourage them to stay with you for the long term. A strategically planned remuneration system can be a powerful tool for engaging your employees in the performance of your business, and for rewarding them for their contribution to its success. It should:

- offer a tangible incentive to employees to achieve targets
- enable people to share in the value they create for the organisation
- assist employees to achieve their own financial and lifestyle objectives.

What is the way you pay your employees telling them?

Transforming employees into committed stakeholders in your business means developing a remuneration system that reflects your organisation's philosophy, objectives and values. What many small and medium-sized businesses don't fully appreciate is how their remuneration practices influence the thinking, behaviour and performance of their staff. The way companies choose to pay their employees communicates the company's values and contributes enormously to the organisation's culture, the type of people it attracts and the results they deliver. So it is important that a remuneration strategy be developed with the organisation's objectives in mind.

Consider the example of a business that only pays its people a standard wage for a standard working day – what is that company saying to its employees? It's saying that nine-to-five thinking is all that's required, and that anything outside of that should come at an extra cost to the company in the form of overtime payments. Do you think that these staff are staying back late or coming in early to get the job done? Or that they're giving their job a moment's thought outside of their standard workday? What about a company that pays bonuses or commissions to individuals for monthly or quarterly results? This communicates the message that it's everyone for him or herself, which encourages a fiercely independent and even competitive organisational culture. The frequency of bonus payments tells employees what timeframe they should be focused on, which can be a valuable tool in encouraging specific short-term results. But without the additional ability to focus people's attention on the longer term, the message is that all they need to be focused on is the next bonus or commission timeframe. In this case you may start to see 'sales-bulking', which is where staff hold and rollover sales from one bonus period into the next, rather than doing more than is necessary to earn a bonus in the current period.

If a company's incentives are only based on sales, then that's what its employees focus on – sometimes at the expense of margin. Their focus would be quite different if rewards were based on maximising gross margin dollars, rather than just gross revenue. And what if a company places an upper limit on the amount of bonus or commission that can be earned? Do you think its employees will continue to drive for results beyond the maximum amount that they will be rewarded for?

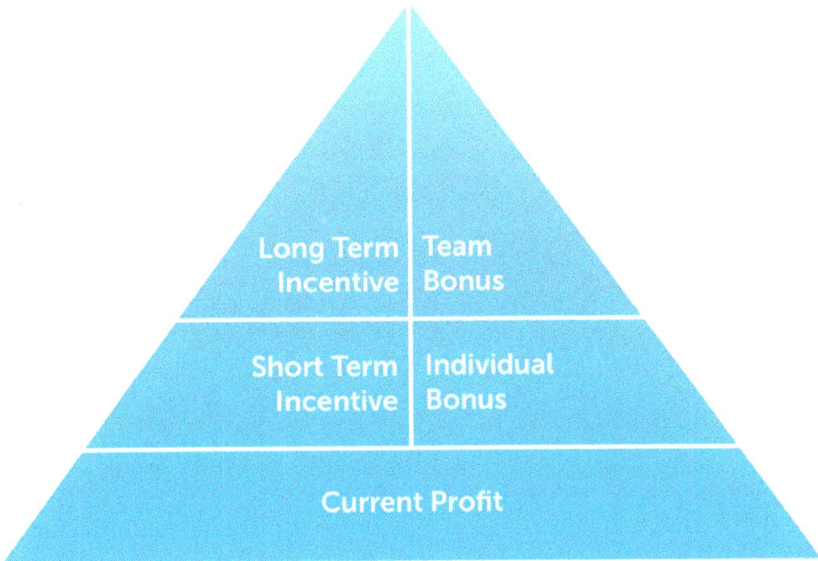

How companies pay people directs how they will think and behave, which impacts the bottom line.

Why a pay packet isn't enough

Employee remuneration is about more than just money – it is about motivation and reward. Remuneration that is comprised of both economic and non-economic benefits will contribute toward increased levels of productivity and morale. One of the most powerful outcomes of a strategically planned remuneration system is that it helps to align your employees' personal and financial goals with your business goals; in other words, it encourages employees to think and act like stakeholders in your business. To achieve this, the ideal mix would include base remuneration, short-term performance bonuses and long-term loyalty bonuses.

Base Pay and Compulsory Employee Benefits

This must be industry-competitive. If you pay less than the rest of the market, you will attract a lower quality of employee, which will be reflected in your operating results. Compulsory employee benefits such as superannuation, annual leave, personal leave and so on can also be enhanced to help position your company as an employer of choice, and will help you retain high-performing staff. For example, company funded superannuation contributions could be increased after a certain number of years' service, or additional paid annual leave offered to long-standing employees.

Discretionary Employee Benefits

These may be financial (such as employee share schemes, employer-funded health insurance or study leave) or non-financial.

Non-financial incentives recognise and reward performance, as well as demonstrating a commitment to employees by assisting them to achieve some of their lifestyle objectives.

Short-term non-financial incentives might include tickets to the theatre or a sporting event, dinner at a restaurant, a weekend away or even just a pat on the back or public acknowledgement for a job well done. They may be awarded to individuals or to teams, to be enjoyed together. Long-term non-financial incentives might include flexible working hours, the option to work from home, the provision of childcare facilities, job sharing and so on.

Performance-Based Pay

This is about rewarding people for their results and should also include both short-term and long-term incentives.

Short-term incentives are designed to influence immediate behaviour to achieve specific short-term goals. They might take the form of cash bonuses, commissions, fringe benefits or anything else that is meaningful to the employee but that does not cost the company unnecessarily in terms of margin.

Long-term incentives provide employees with a vested interest in increasing the value of the organisation. In the US and UK, long-term incentives make up between 50 and 60% of an executive's annual remuneration. There is a growing global trend toward decreasing the percentage of fixed remuneration and increasing the percentage of remuneration at risk in both the short and long term. With high performing staff, linking higher remuneration to results is a win/win for both the business and the employee – the sky is literally the limit for both. Many long-term incentive schemes include a vesting period, often up to five years, which means that the employee must remain with the company for a longer period of time before he or she can enjoy the full benefits of the scheme.

Examples of Discretionary Employee Benefits

- generous long service leave provisions
- shopping vouchers
- family dinners, movies or holidays
- one-off thank you gifts
- office lunches
- afternoons off
- contributions to nominated charities
- birthday gift vouchers
- reimbursement of study fees
- study leave or flexible hours for study

- payment of children's school fees
- funded health insurance
- additional superannuation contributions
- flexible hours
- work from home
- dry-cleaning pick up and drop off at the office
- child care facilities
- dependant care days
- job sharing
- commuting assistance
- casual dress days
- health promotion programs
- reimbursement of gym fees
- club memberships
- personal legal, accounting and financial planning services.

Base Remuneration
Salaries and Wages
Other Benefits

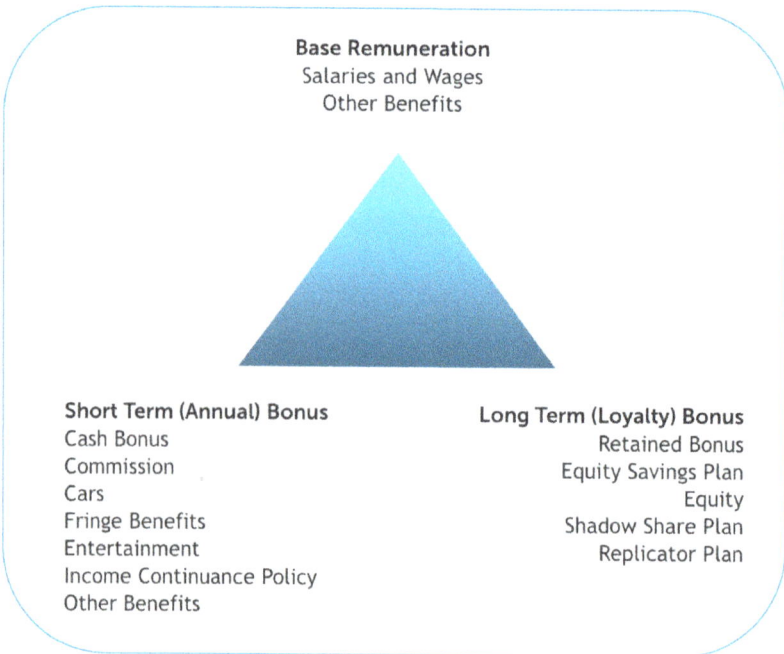

Short Term (Annual) Bonus
Cash Bonus
Commission
Cars
Fringe Benefits
Entertainment
Income Continuance Policy
Other Benefits

Long Term (Loyalty) Bonus
Retained Bonus
Equity Savings Plan
Equity
Shadow Share Plan
Replicator Plan

Successful remuneration strategies are those that attract and retain employees by rewarding high performance over both the short and long term.

Employee incentive scheme tips and traps

As much as they can offer great benefits to employers and employees alike, remuneration systems that are not properly developed or implemented can also act as a disincentive. At their most ineffective, such systems can cause a loss of trust, loss of engagement or loss of faith in the organisation. You can avoid making a mess of your system by working with expert advisers and following these simple rules.
Effective remuneration systems are:

Simple
The system must be well thought-out and easy for staff to understand, so that they know how it applies to them.

Applicable
While the levels of remuneration and reward may differ, the process should apply consistently to all employees. Employees should only benefit from a positive outcome over which they have had some input, and they should not be penalised for a negative outcome over which they had no influence.

Reliable
Once the system is established and has been communicated to staff, avoid making unnecessary or frequent changes to it.

Transparent
The system should be communicated in plain English and relevant information should be disclosed on a regular basis, in a format that is easily understood by all staff.

Performance indicators and measurement are a critical aspect of any incentive plan. The way staff performance will be assessed must be clearly defined and communicated so that there is no room for ambiguity or dispute. As with the system itself, the way that performance is measured will have a direct impact on the day-to-day activities and major business decisions made by participating employees, so again it is essential that the system be developed around the organisation's objectives and desired culture. All performance indicators must be able to be measured objectively, preferably using systems and/or data, particularly where a subjective performance appraisal is a factor in determining an employee's eligibility for a performance bonus.

Supported

Once it is launched, the system must be fully supported by the company's owners and managers.

It's not all about the money

While financial and lifestyle goals are key motivators for people, most of us are also substantially driven by intrinsic rewards: job satisfaction, the opportunity to rise up and meet new challenges, recognition for a job well done. So, while generous remuneration and employee incentive schemes are important, they're just one component of what must be an integrated and satisfying work experience that will help your organisation to retain the best people over the long term.

Other important aspects of staff retention include:
- creating a positive and supportive work environment
- recognising and catering to individual differences matching the right people with the right jobs
- using realistic and achievable goals and targets to challenge people
- implementing training, programs for professional development and career advancement.

Ladder to Equity

While the research undoubtedly shows an increase in employees looking for equity in the business they work for – Australia lags behind on the world stage in providing a mechanism to achieve this. According to recent research in both the United States and Europe, a little over 30% of employees have some kind of equity interest in the business they work for, while in Australia that number is around 8%. A simple mechanism to manage the transition through various stages is the issue. It is not simple, nor smart, to simply take an employee and provide them with equity – and thus the ladder becomes important.

As Warren Buffet says:
"Employees are keen to climb the ladder to equity – but someone needs to provide the ladder."

Progressive staged approach:
- Employee Earnings – Earning (salary/wage/hourly rates etc.) – this is where most employees start (and stay).
- Income Model – The first step on the ladder then is to boost that income and this is quite common. We often see companies paying bonuses, commissions on sales, incentives etc. to increase an employee's income. This is a great step to link performance with reward.
- Profit Share – Most equity plans begin with this simple step and in fact many end at this step. Simply providing a share of profits to employees is a great additional incentive as they are directly rewarded as a result of the financial performance of the company in the same way that a business owner typically would be. This step changes the focus from personal to team performance.
- Equity – While there are many equity plans available, our models provide a formal structured mechanism to incorporate profit share, equity and control into any business succession plan. This allows employees to transition into an equity ownership position within the business they work for and encourages long-term strategic thinking.

- Control – Often this step is never utilised though on occasion has substantial benefits in terms of succession, not only in terms of ownership but also of business management. Ultimately, control means that employees can be transitioned through the earlier four stages and end up in a position of control. This may mean that they take over general management or become CEO of the company. It may also be that they end up with a seat on the board at some future date however, this step is not to be rushed.

If managed correctly, the ladder is a great methodology to identify opportunities to progressively transition employees to think and act like business owners and motivate key employees in the long term. Note however that the transition should be managed carefully with KPIs and performance criteria to proceed up the ladder. Such plans can fall over without logical steps listed out for employees or where businesses miss steps trying to fast track progression.How can you get your staff to think and act more like business owners?

How can you get your staff to think and act more like business owners?

"Employee ownership is world-changing.
It is the way ahead... in the global economy.
It reflects that human capital is becoming more
important than physical assets...
The global economy will succeed when
employees feel a stake in the business."

Gordon Brown MP
Ex-Chancellor of the Exchequer

There are many more interesting and creative options for employee incentive schemes than just paying bonuses. Participation in the equity of a business is a key component of an effective reward system. While fixed remuneration rewards the individual for performing his or her duties; and incentive plans help to direct a person's activities, decisions and behaviours toward the achievement of predetermined short-term goals; a share plan is an essential tool for aligning the employee's personal goals with the business's goals in the longer term.

Back in July 2015, the Federal Government introduced new measures to encourage and promote the use of ESOPs.

The Government recognised that ESOPs benefit both employers and employees by:

- aligning their interests and goals
- enabling employees to directly benefit when their employer does well, and
- enabling employers to benefit from a more committed workforce.

Former Telstra CEO David Thodey said "There's no better way to tune people in to creating shareholder value than to make them shareholders... I do know it gave our people more understanding and a sense of responsibility for what was going on in the company... In my view, it's a win-win."

In November 2018, the Government announced further proposed measures to the employee share scheme.

The proposals aim to simplify and extend the current regime by:

- creating a dedicated exemption for disclosure, licensing, advertising and on-sale obligations under the Corporations Act 2001
- increasing the value limit of eligible financial products that can be offered in a 12-month period from $5000 per employee to $10,000 per employee
- expanding employee share schemes to include contribution plans, where an employee can make a monetary contribution to acquire eligible financial products, and

- allowing small businesses to offer employee share schemes without publicly disclosing commercially sensitive financial information unless they are otherwise obligated to do.

Share plans that first provide for the owners to receive an equitable return (profit) on their risk and capital, and then allocate a percentage of additional profits to a pool for employees to share in, vastly improve the profits of an organisation, while promoting teamwork, common goals and group achievements. Strategically planned and executed employee share plans can also help businesses and their staff to achieve a number of other goals, for example, succession planning, capital retention, wealth creation and asset protection. See below for more detail.

Succession Planning

According to the 2018 Family Business Survey, published by Family Business Australia together with KPMG Australia and the University of South Australia, the average age of a family business owner today is between 55 and 64 years, and 60% plan to retire within the next five years. Over the next decade, the retirement of family business owners will see the transfer of approximately $4.2 trillion in wealth, which surely must make succession planning one of the most significant issues currently facing small business owners.

Employee share ownership schemes can significantly assist in the transition of business ownership. For example:

- In the case of a management buy-out, the ability for staff to acquire equity (through an employee incentive scheme) can facilitate the transfer of ownership over a period of time.
- In the case of an external sale, an employee incentive scheme can help to increase the value of the business; prospective buyers will be prepared to invest more in a business where the employees' financial interests are aligned with those of the employer. (You'll find more on succession planning in my book, Enjoy It.)

Capital Retention

The opportunity to raise capital from within the business rather than from external investors or lenders, can be an attractive option which enables control of the organisation to remain in-house, while giving employees the opportunity to share in equity and profits.

Wealth Creation

Contributions to investment vehicles created as part of an employee share ownership scheme can offer employees the ability to invest pre-tax dollars, which is a unique opportunity for wealth creation that is particularly attractive to people who have the financial capacity to save on a regular basis.

Asset Protection

The use of trusts as investment vehicles can provide asset protection for both employer and employee. In the event that either the employer or a participating employee experiences financial difficulties, to the extent that funds invested in an employee incentive scheme are held within a trust (rather than by the employer), those funds will be protected from bankruptcy trustees. (For more about asset protection, request a copy of my book, Protect It.)

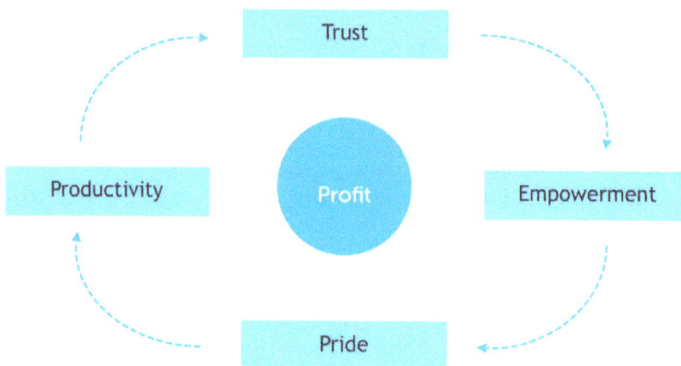

The primary objective of an employee share ownership scheme is to create a structure within which your employees' lifestyle and financial goals are aligned with your business objectives. The result? A cohesive and committed team that is single-minded about working toward, and sharing in, the benefits of a successful and profitable business.

There are a number of different employee share and equity vehicles commonly used, and each has its advantages and disadvantages. We will take a brief look at these in the next chapter, then introduce you to an entirely new type of employee equity plan, called the Peak Performance Trust (PPT). It captures the best elements of each of the following options in one unique trust that is only offered by Succession Plus.

Common employee equity and share ownership plans

"However beautiful the strategy,
you should occasionally look at the results."

Winston Churchill

The most common employee equity and share ownership plans are:
- Start-up plans
- Option plans
- Replicator employee share plans
- Public employee savings plans
- Deferred tax plans.

Let's discuss each of these generally below.

Start-up ESOP Plans

These plans have been introduced by the Government as part of the Government Industry Innovation and Competitiveness Agenda and are simple to set up and use. They also have significant tax advantages for participants with no upfront tax, no tax at vesting and no tax on exercise.

Participants are generally only taxed on disposal of shares or options and with 50% CGT discount.

The Start-up ESOP plans are restricted to businesses that meet all of the following conditions for **employers**:
- Not listed on public exchange
- Aggregated turnover less than $50m
- Less than 10 years old
- Australian resident taxpayer.

Shares must be available to 75% of employees with more than three years' service. In addition, **employees** must also meet the following criteria:
- Must collectively own less than 10% of shares (and voting rights)Must be employed by holding company or subsidiary or subsidiary
- May only receive a 15% or lower discount on shares
- Must hold shares for at least 3 years.

The Option Plan

This is a flexible plan that enables small companies to provide equity to principals and key employees. It is best used as a vehicle to reward employee performance and to align employee and company goals. It is delivered by a simple and effective option contract and integrates both short and long-term employee incentives.

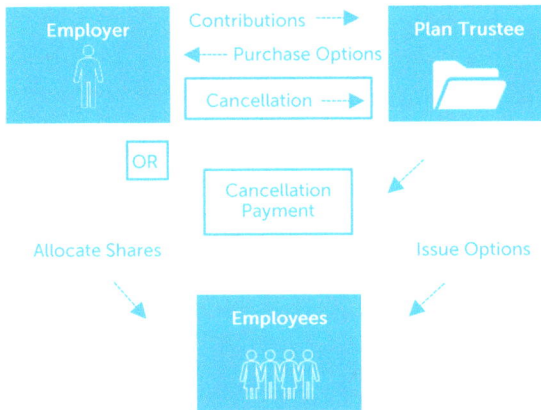

The Option Plan	
Advantages	**Disadvantages**
• Flexible – facilitates virtually any vesting contingency • Easy to administer • Tax effective, but not tax driven • Efficient and effective delivery of after-tax equity benefits • Administration costs are fully tax deductible to employer • Funding of realised benefits is fully deductible to employer • Employees are eligible for Capital Gains Tax discount on gains • No prospectus obligations	• Options granted to employees are difficult (if not impossible) to value • Options are generally illiquid • Can be difficult for employees that have no experience in trading options to understand

Replicator Share Company

This is an employee share plan through which equity can be provided to any or all employees of any sized company. This option has the capacity to offer a large range of investment choices, and is designed to provide employees with the benefits of investment in assets that replicate the value of the underlying business.

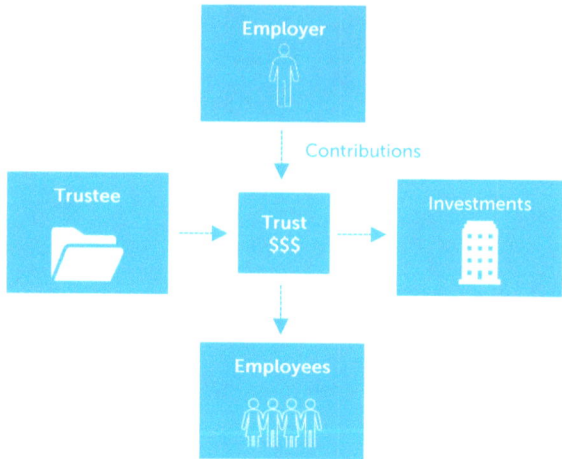

Replicator Share Company	
Advantages	**Disadvantages**
• Flexible – facilitates virtually any vesting contingency • Can provide a range of investment options • Offered on a fully administered basis • Easy to understand and communicate • Tax effective, but not tax driven • Efficient and effective delivery of after-tax equity benefits • Administration costs are fully tax deductible to employer • Funding of realised benefits is fully deductible to employer • Employees are eligible for Capital Gains Tax discount on gains • Established wrap-around prospectus precedents	• Difficult to accurately replicate the value of the business • Liquidity is uncertain and variable

Public Employee Savings Plan

The most effective savings plan for employees of public sector and not-for-profit organisations. This plan is designed to offer employees the opportunity to access the same equity and investment opportunities that are generally available in private sector employee share plans.

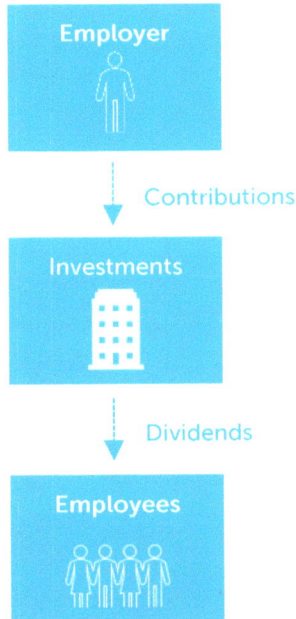

Public Employee Savings Plan	
Advantages	**Disadvantages**
• Flexible – facilitates most vesting contingencies • Can provide a range of investment options • Offered on a fully administered basis • Tax effective, but not tax driven • Contributions taxed as salary • Employees are eligible for Capital Gains Tax discount on gains	• Difficult to match equity/income to employee performance • Liquidity is uncertain

Deferred Tax Plans – Div 83 A

Deferred taxation means that the employee is taxed on the value of a share or right they acquire under an Employee Share Scheme (ESS interest) at the 'deferred taxing point' (on the market value at that time) rather than at the time they acquire the ESS interest.

Under the current ESS rules, deferred taxation automatically applies to a qualifying ESS interest if either:

- there is a 'real risk of forfeiture' of the ESS interest under the scheme, or
- the scheme is a qualifying salary sacrifice arrangement.

Deferred taxation will not apply (and the employee will therefore be taxed up-front) if the employee and/or their 'associates':

- holds a beneficial interest in more than 10% of the shares in the company (which specifically includes shares that the employee can acquire under an ESS interest that is a right to acquire such shares), or
- is in a position to cast, or control the casting of, more than 10% of the votes that may be cast at a general meeting of the company (which, again, includes the voting power attached to any shares the employee can acquire under an ESS interest that is a right to acquire such shares.

The taxing point only arises when the right is exercised and:

- there is no real risk that, under the conditions of the scheme, that the employee will forfeit or lose the share acquired on exercise (other than by disposing of it), and
- there are no genuine restrictions under the scheme on disposal of the share.

For all ESS interests, the maximum deferral period under s 83A-120(6) will be 15 years after acquisition of the ESS interest.

The ultimate employee equity ownership plan

"The truth is that profit-sharing doesn't create employee involvement, it requires it."

Ricardo Semler

Introduction

One of the most innovative vehicles through which to provide employee share ownership is a customised Peak Performance Trust (PPT) – a type of trust that has been developed by, and is only available through, Succession Plus.

The PPT has been developed specifically to meet the needs of small to medium-sized businesses. If there's any business sector that truly benefits from having employees that are motivated to think and act more like business owners, it's SMEs. But until now employee incentive vehicles like the ones we've just looked at have been designed for large corporates – they're complicated, expensive, difficult to establish and administer, and largely inappropriate for smaller privately-owned companies.

After twenty years of working with small and medium-sized businesses and understanding their needs, we developed the PPT to offer smaller companies a tool that delivers all the benefits of a sophisticated employee incentive scheme, but without the expense or complexity. The PPT is simple, effective and good value for the benefits it brings.

CPA Australia's *In the Black* magazine described PPTs as an 'ingenious funding mechanism' for exit strategies, the PPT links increased profits to performance payments made into a trust on behalf of employees, building an employee's stake in the business.

With a PPT, the employer creates an investment trust into which it makes contributions on behalf of, and for the benefit of, its employees. It makes a commitment to investing a predetermined amount of money into the trust on a regular basis, contingent upon participating employees achieving predetermined performance outcomes. As the profits increase, so too does the percentage share that employees can benefit from. If profits are not increased, then no further allocation of funds is made to the PPT.

The benefits of participating in a PPT for both the employer and employee can be considerable. This, unlike any other type of employee incentive tool, truly ties the employee's financial and lifestyle goals to the performance of the company. It is the ultimate 'golden handcuff' for your high performing staff.

From employees to company landlords

One of my clients used a PPT to enable its employees to buy the business's premises. Every time the team achieved sales of $1 million, the employer would transfer $100,000 into the trust. A board of trustees was appointed to manage the trust and make decisions about how to invest and distribute the income. The board comprised myself as the independent expert, a legal expert, a staff-elected representative and the owner of the company. When the trust decided to buy the building, all of the employees became joint landlords of the business. The business now pays rent to the trust, from which all employees receive a dividend. Staff turnover in this organisation has dropped to an all-time low, and as an unexpected bonus staff now take an extra measure of care and pride in their facilities. Ten or twenty years from now, the value of the asset will have increased dramatically and the staff will continue to receive benefits from the income of the trust.

Using PPTs to fund succession planning

One of the best ways that a PPT can benefit the business is to provide a facility to fund an ongoing succession planning arrangement – whereby money set aside within the trust is used to fund the purchase of a proportion of the business. Because the purchase is directly linked to the performance of the business, it becomes largely self-funding. This can also add to the value of the company because it can clearly be demonstrated to potential buyers that the employees' future incomes are directly linked to the future performance of the company.

PPTs can fund succession planning in a couple of different ways:

- The simplest way is for the PPT to simply lend funds on a commercial basis to an employee (or employees) for the purpose of enabling them to acquire shares in the business (Option Two on page 42).

- Alternatively, funds within the trust can be used to purchase shares within the trust, thereby giving all employees who are unit holders an indirect interest in the business entity. This option also has the benefit of involving all staff in ownership of the trust, which becomes the primary shareholder in the business. It can greatly simplify the business ownership structure; rather than having a number of individual shareholders. This can lead to minority shareholder issues as well as cost and compliance problems, the trust becomes the majority shareholder and the employees become unit holders within the trust. So the benefits of share ownership can be achieved without complicated ownership structures (see Options 1A and 1B on pages 39–41).

As mentioned previously, PPTs are especially advantageous from a taxation point of view when used solely for the purpose of funding succession within the business because they become FBT exempt. See Part 2 for a detailed example of how these benefits apply.

Benefits of PPTs

The benefits of a PPT in succession planning include the following:
- gives the company a competitive advantage in recruiting, motivating and retaining high performance staff
- affordable for the business
- encourages ongoing profit improvement through rewards linked to performance
- tax effective for both the business and participating employees
- reflects and influences the values and culture of the business
- supports employee development
- rewards employees who make a substantial contribution to the business
- reflects different individual motivations
- is easily understood, controlled and managed
- is appropriate for both the long and short term
- complies with all current and likely Australian taxation and legal requirements

SUCCESSION+

- assists in funding succession planning and new business opportunities
- assists employees to achieve their financial and lifestyle goals.

Features of a PPT

The PPT has the following features:

- An employer or employee makes a request to set up a Peak Performance Trust (PPT)
- The PPT will have a corporate trustee which will manage the affairs of the PPT
- Both the employer and one or more employees will be able to make contributions to the PPT
- Each employee will be invited to join the trust based on predetermined selection criteria and will be allocated units in the trust
- Typically, the employer will agree to make a contribution to the trust annually based on a profit share formula
- The trustee (based on the rules outlined in the trust deed) will have strictly limited investment powers which will restrict the PPT to only investing in shares in the employer entity (or holding company)
- The PPT units will convey the same rights as owning direct shares to the unit holders, (i.e. 1 unit = 1 share)
- Under the terms of the trust deed all employee units which are the result of an employer contribution are subject to the disqualifying events and disqualifying discounts (see pages 62 and 63)
- Income (i.e. dividends paid by the employer company to the PPT) of the PPT, must be distributed to unit holders on an annual basis, though this may happen more frequently, based on the number of units held by the employee.

Who can participate in a Peak Performance Trust?

Each PPT is tailored to the needs of each individual business and the participation criteria can be varied accordingly, however, there will usually be two qualifying criteria for participating employees:

- an employee must have worked for the employer for an initial period (for example, twelve months) before being invited to participate as a unit holder in the PPT;
- an employee must continue to work for that employer for a designated period of time before realising the value of the investment (for example, employees who leave in the first two years may only be able to extract 25 per cent of their investment; after three years, 50 per cent; and after four years, 75 per cent, and so on).

A PPT can be structured in the following two different ways, depending on the needs and objectives of the company:

- Option One creates a structure designed specifically for succession planning by transitioning ownership of equity in the company to key employees over a period of time. Using a PPT to fund succession planning offers significant tax advantages, which we explain in detail in Part 2
- Option Two creates a PPT designed for investment in external vehicles.

Generally, PPTs are taxed in the following ways:
- Contributions to the PPT are not taxable income of the PPT
- Income received by the PPT (dividends from the employer entity) are income and must be distributed to unitholders
- Expenses incurred in managing the PPT (for example, bank fees) are deductible to the PPT.

As mentioned previously, the Government has just proposed the following measures in November 2018 to simplify and extend the current regime by:

- creating a dedicated exemption for disclosure, licensing, advertising and on-sale obligations under the Corporations Act 2001
- increasing the value limit of eligible financial products that can be offered in a 12-month period from $5000 per employee to $10,000 per employee
- expanding employee share schemes to include contribution plans, where an employee can make a monetary contribution to acquire eligible financial products, and
- allowing small businesses to offer employee share schemes without publicly disclosing commercially sensitive financial information unless they are otherwise obligated to do.

How the PPT works

Here is an overview of how both PPTs work:

Option One: PPT for internal investment

When it comes to designing a PPT for internal investment (or succession planning), there are two options. Option 1A provides for indirect, or pooled ownership, where the PPT invests in shares in the company and unit holders of the PPT (selected employees) become indirect equity holders in the company. Option 1B enables selected employees to borrow funds from the PPT (or an external funder/bank) for direct investment in company shares in their own names.

Option 1A: Indirect Ownership

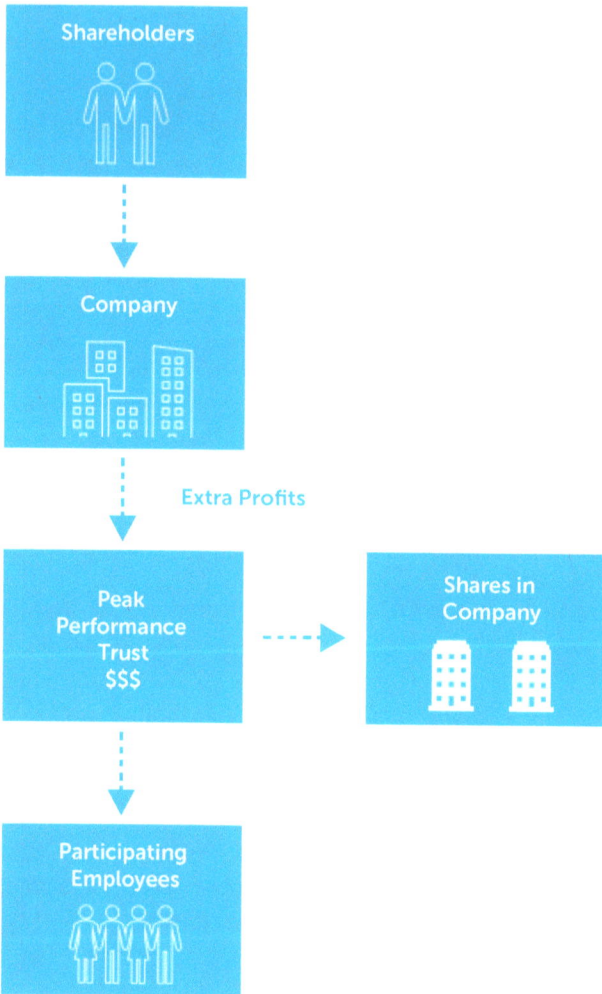

Option 1B: Direct Ownership

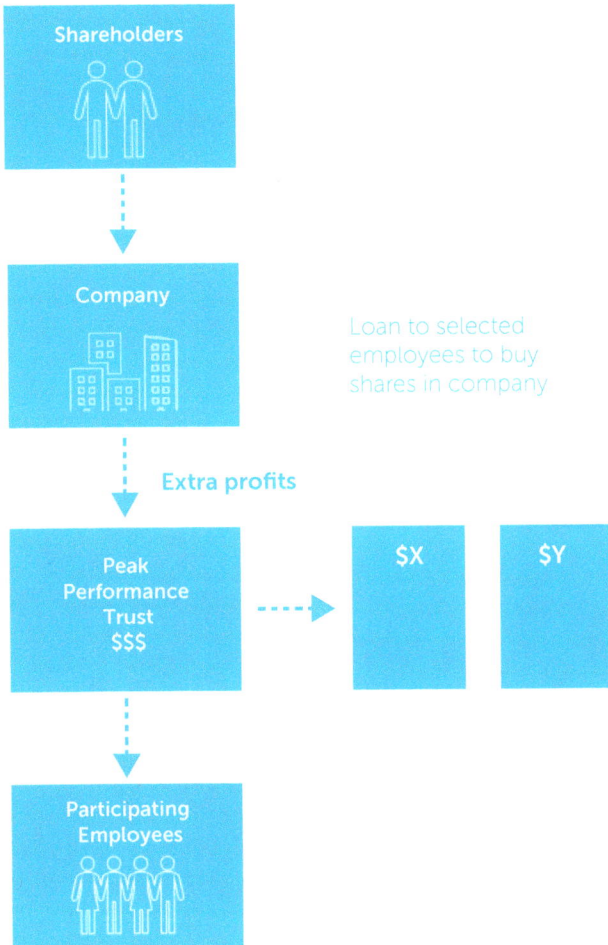

Option Two: PPT for external investment

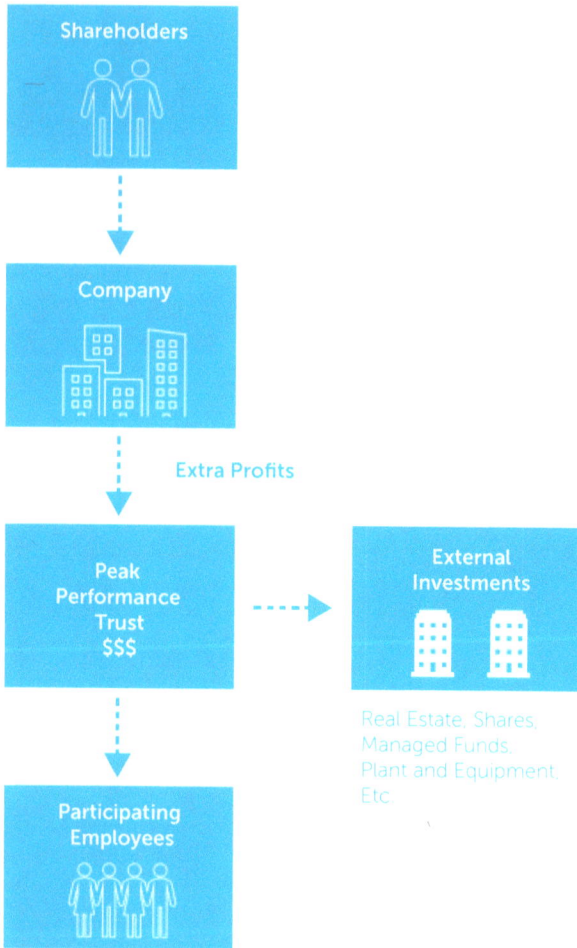

Six easy steps to implementing a PPT in your business

Step One: Identify Key Employees and KPIs

The first step in the process is to identify:

- which employees you want to include within the PPT
- which aspects of their performance you plan to focus on, and therefore gear the trust toward improving.

It is preferable to include as many people in the organisation as possible, within predetermined eligibility criteria. The criteria should specify a minimum period of employment, the vesting arrangements and what is to happen when an employee leaves the organisation. Refer to 'Employee Participation' on page 59 for more about employee eligibility considerations.

Because the PPT is such a flexible structure, it can be customised to measure and reward different performance criteria in different businesses – so it is important to determine which aspects of individual and overall performance you wish to focus on and reward. No more than two or three KPIs are recommended so as to not overcomplicate the process for either yourself or your employees.

While the primary focus of a PPT should always be increased profitability, you can also incorporate a range of other performance metrics, including some that aren't even financial. For example, you could include performance measurements of:

- sales
- customer
- complaints
- billable hours
- punctuality.

The PPT's flexibility enables it to be used to measure and reward both individual and team performance. One of my clients, a mortgage lender, rewards its mortgage broking team leaders first on the profitability of the business overall, second on the number of loans settled by his or her team, and finally on the number of loans he or she individually signs up. This multi-focused approach not only creates incentives for individual performance, but also for strong team performance, and contributes to the development of highly cohesive teams that are single-mindedly focused on achieving results that allow everyone to benefit.

Step Two: Financial Modelling

Next, it is important to review and model the financial performance of your business in order to ensure that the KPIs you have chosen are appropriate and will actually drive increased profit. For example, many businesses nominate 'sales volume' as a KPI, but all this does is encourage staff to discount prices to increase sales. The impact on the business is a decreasing rather than increasing gross profit margin.

The best place to begin financial modelling is by looking at your business's current profit drivers. Your accountant should be able to identify what factors within your remuneration system and fee structure significantly affect the profitability of your business, and these are the areas that the PPT should focus on to motivate improvements. With or without a PPT, all businesses should model their financial performance and identify their key profit drivers in order to understand what actually influences their bottom line. If you get this wrong you'll be focusing on the wrong things; add a PPT to the mix and you'll be providing incentives for your staff to focus on improving the wrong outcomes.

Rigorous financial modelling should also be undertaken to determine the level of profitability within the business, to identify what level of bonus payment can be made to the PPT while still allowing the business's profitability to improve. It is a useless exercise to simply give away all of the increased profit.

As part of the PPT implementation program, we prepare a detailed financial model that examines each of these factors, and shows the effect of the PPT at various levels of performance. This allows business owners to determine exactly what their business's financial position will be post implementation. The following is an example of a strategic forecast model.

This following graph is from the case study used throughout my book "Enjoy It". This book provides you with a step by step guide to business succession and exit planning. The business in the case study is called Smith Engineering Pty Ltd with Jane and John being the owners. Rod has worked for them for many years. The following graph highlights how the employees (Rod and other managers) benefit following the introduction of employee incentive schemes, with an increase in equity in the business for employees, while there is a decrease in the owner's share (Jane and John) over a five-year period.

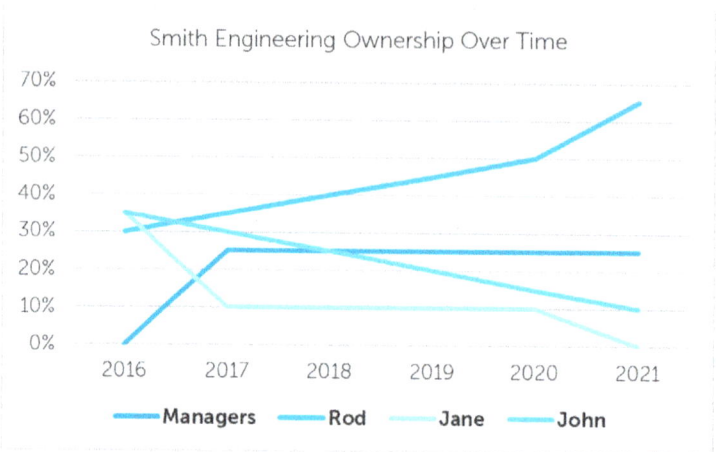

Smith Engineering Ownership Over Time

	2016	2017	2018	2019	2020	2021
Managers	0%	25%	25%	25%	25%	25%
Rod	30%	35%	40%	45%	50%	65%
Jane	35%	10%	10%	10%	10%	0%
John	35%	30%	25%	20%	15%	10%

Step Three: Employee Education

There is little point in setting up any type of bonus profit share plan if employees don't understand how it works, or if they become discouraged by the plan because of a lack of communication and transparency. A structured program of internal communications to launch and report on the PPT on an ongoing basis is essential.

When first introducing the PPT, staff seminars are ideal. The objective of these is to educate staff about what the PPT is, how it works, what performance measures it is focusing on improving and so on. This usually takes place over two or three separate sessions designed to first help staff understand the concept of the PPT, and then the detail of the company's specific plan. Staff also receive a handbook that clearly outlines the operation of the PPT, the legal mechanisms behind it, their rights and obligations as participants, what they can expect on an ongoing basis in terms of reporting and communication, and so on.

Step Four: Introducing the PPT

In preparation for its introduction, the necessary legal documents are drawn up and the trust is created. Appropriate communications to all stakeholders are again important during this phase. It is vital to keep everyone abreast of the implementation, and what they need to do in preparation for the launch.

We often discover that clients do not have many of the necessary systems or documents in place in readiness for the introduction of a PPT. These include up-to-date employment agreements (in many companies they are old or non-existent), and salary, wage and accounting software appropriate to manage the PPT (often it's not even adequate for the pre-PPT requirements of the business). We also often see gaps within businesses' budgeting and financial modelling – many business owners simply don't have a handle on their existing financial arrangements and structure, or the costings and KPIs that drive the performance of their business. There is little point in adding new and more complicated systems on top of an already struggling infrastructure, so these issues must be addressed prior to the introduction of the PPT.

Step Five: Integrating the PPT

Many business owners have experienced the impact of major reforms such as the introduction of the superannuation guarantee charge and the GST, and they understand that changes in the way their businesses operate require staff to be re-trained, new systems to be put into place, documentation to be updated, and in some cases, equipment upgraded. While integrating a PPT is nowhere near as challenging as these major changes, it will require a new way of doing things in order to ensure that the maximum benefit is derived for both the business and its employees.

The PPT is a separate legal structure with its own rights and obligations in terms of taxation compliance and regulatory reporting, and therefore needs to have its own separate set of accounts, tax returns and so on. Accounting software programs such as Xero can easily be set up to calculate, manage and report on the PPT. One of the duties of the board of trustees is to ensure that all the compliance issues within the fund are managed, and that returns and documents are lodged correctly and on time, to ensure that the fund is fully compliant.

For the PPT to achieve its ultimate purpose, not only do the systems, administration and compliance issues need to be managed, but the fund needs to be fully-integrated into the business. So, for example, when potential new employees are introduced to the business, they should be told what the PPT is, why it works and how it can potentially benefit them as a key aspect of the company's employment offering.

I have one client who successfully uses a PPT in conjunction with a succession plan to actively attract employees into the business, and he finds it a distinct advantage in positioning his business as an employer of choice. It is also a valuable lever to incentivise employees rather than having to rely solely on continual salary increases to reward and retain staff.

Step Six: Ongoing Communication and Management

Ongoing communication and management of the PPT is essential. The management of a PPT and its associated payments is very similar to the way superannuation is managed, so we advise clients to handle their PPT in the same way as their superannuation.

Employees should receive quarterly statements outlining the fund's performance, the contributions they've received, and the investments that the trust has undertaken on their behalf. This allows employees to actually see the tangible benefit of having the PPT, and it becomes more than just some vague concept that they are not really aware of or engaged with, as is often the case with other option and share plans.

It is equally important that participating employees have representation on the board of trustees and that all participants are informed about, if not engaged in, major investment decisions. For example, I have one client whose PPT has purchased the business premises. All participating employees were involved in that purchase decision and now have a stake in the performance of that investment.

Following its establishment, ongoing administration is an important part of managing your PPT to ensure compliance with taxation law and that the benefits to both your business and the trust's unit holders are maximised. This process involves us staying actively involved in helping you and your financial managers and advisers to make your PPT work.

Your PPT team will also include:

Accountant

Your company accountant will be involved in the process at several stages and will also need to prepare the trust's annual accounts and returns.

Legal Counsel

Preparation of legal documentation is included as part of the establishment of the trust, but we recommend that you seek advice on these documents from your lawyer.

Investment Adviser

You may decide to engage the services of an appropriately qualified investment adviser to manage the trust's funds. We can recommend suitable organisations for your consideration.

PPTs in action

These examples of PPTs come from case studies of actual clients, the details of their PPT arrangements are accurate, but their names have been omitted to ensure their privacy.

PPT for specific-purpose investment – 'XYZ Pty Ltd'

The key issues for this company were funding for acquisition of tools and equipment, which can be expensive in the building and construction industry, and the ongoing issue of equipment being damaged and 'lost'.

This company could also choose to purchase the buildings from which it operates, or its fleet of vehicles from its PPT, again making the staff who use them and participate in the PPT indirect owners of the asset, thereby giving them a vested interest in ensuring the asset's maintenance and upkeep. There are no restrictions from either a legal or taxation perspective as to the PPT's ability to buy key business assets and lease them back to the operating entity.

PPT for shares-only investment – 'ABC Financial Planning Pty Ltd'

In the case of this client, the investment strategy for the PPT is simple – it will only ever purchase direct shares in the business, thereby giving participating employees an indirect ownership of the business's equity. Its staff receive dividends and a bonus reward based on the profit performance of the practice. If the practice was to ever be sold, the PPT would benefit from the capital sale, and indirectly, the employees would receive part of that capital gain.

Based on this simple strategy, the value of the PPT automatically replicates any change in the value of the business, therefore employees directly benefit (or otherwise) from any change in value which is largely driven by profit performance and is something that the employees can directly influence.

PPT via independent advice – 'Hands Off Pty Ltd'

While this business saw the benefits of enabling its employees to share in the company's profitability it had no expertise, and no desire to acquire expertise, in the management of the trust.

On our advice, they engaged an external financial planner who was qualified to manage the investments on their behalf. The planner advised participating employees on the different types of investments available, and the client provided specific direction as to the risk profile, income requirements and long term goals of the trust. The planner invested the

PPT funds in listed shares and property trusts, giving it exposure to the equities markets and property sector, and at the same time managing diversity and ongoing income to the fund.

The costs of providing the financial planning advice were carried by the trust (not the employees) and the returns generated over several years added significant value to the funds contributed to the trust by the business.

PPT for succession planning – 'New Partners Pty Ltd'

This professional practice, like many others, had an issue with being able to fund key staff into partnership. The staff members most commonly identified as having partnership potential typically didn't have the financial resources to purchase a share in the practice, because in most cases people are approached about partnership in their early thirties when they are often getting married, having children and buying houses, a range of life circumstances that don't usually add up to having funds available to purchase equity in a professional practice.

The PPT in this case was specifically designed to provide succession funding. The funds were invested in secure investment products until suitable employees were identified for partnership, and it then loaned them the money under a commercial loan agreement. This not only enables selected staff to accept partnership opportunities, but it also shows "rising stars" that this is an option that they could potentially benefit from in the future.

Offering this type of funding opportunity to staff has not only increased the value of the practice, but it also provides a distinct differentiator with which to attract new senior staff.

• PART 2

Technical guide to PPTs

The inner workings of a PPT

The fundamental principle of the PPT is to reward profit increasing performance, so it is imperative that bonus payments into the trust only occur when profits have increased and individual performance against predetermined criteria has been achieved.

A PPT should be used as a true bonus-earning opportunity for staff, not as a substitute for less than competitive base remuneration. Standard rates of pay for all personnel should be benchmarked against industry averages on an annual basis, and assessed against other internal pay rates every two years. With the introduction of a PPT, apart from short term incentive opportunities, other discretionary payments to employees should be discontinued.

Bonus Payment Formula

A minimum target is determined, based on financial modelling for your business.

Once the minimum target is achieved, the company contributes a predetermined amount (for example, 20%) of any additional profits to the bonus pool (provided that the payments do not force the company into loss). If the target is not achieved, no bonus payment is made. When determining whether the target has been achieved or not, total turnover and participating profit margin should be calculated so that it reflects actual net collected income and profit – that is, discounts, refunds and bad debts should be deducted from the calculation of gross revenue.

The board of directors may, at its discretion, vary the percentage controls if it decides that this is in the best interests of all employees.

Bonus funds are allocated to a pool each quarter, after the relevant financial and individual performance assessments have taken place. Funds from the bonus pool are then invested in the PPT.

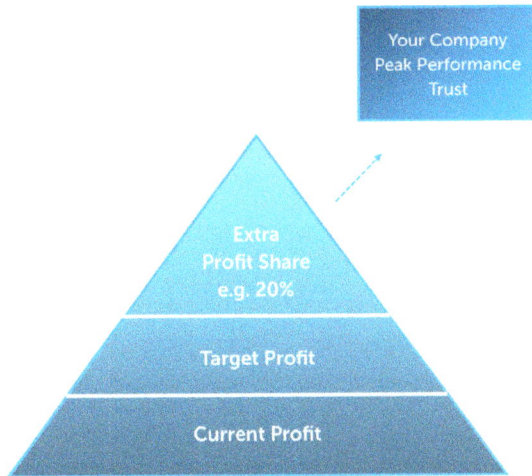

Once minimum gross profit targets are achieved, the company contributes a predetermined amount of any additional profits to the bonus pool.

The Trustee

The PPT is managed by a corporate trustee, which has wide investment powers. It is recommended that the directors of the corporate trustee include:

- two employee representatives (employees that are participating in the plan)
- one employer representative (a director or owner of the company) and an independent adviser (accountant, lawyer or representative of Succession Plus).

At the discretion of the trustee, monies held in the trust may be invested in:

- external investments, such as listed shares and managed funds, or
- internal investments, such as the acquisition of plant, equipment or real property associated with the business; loans to selected employees to enable them to purchase shares in the company; or acquisition of company shares thereby enabling unit holders to participate indirectly in ownership of the business.

Funds within a PPT should be invested with three key objectives in mind:

1. to provide a good return to unit holders (that is, the employees of the business)
2. to provide a benefit to the business overall, which will in turn add value for all employees and unit holders, and
3. to align the interests of employees and owners.

Income is distributed to participating employees annually, based on the number of units held at the beginning of each financial year, and on how much those contributions have earned during the year.

Information about the performance of the organisation and the PPT should be made available regularly (ideally monthly), together with communication from management explaining where improvements can be made. This information should be displayed prominently throughout the organisation, via a screen saver, intranet, internal newsletter or on a noticeboard as the model on the next page. Regular and easy-to-understand performance reports enable staff to become engaged in the process of measuring, managing and hopefully improving business performance.

A common misconception among business owners is that they need to provide extensive information, but that's not the case. It is far more effective for staff to understand and be focused on improving the business's key financial drivers. One of my clients, a sales-based business, simply reports on sales versus targets, which is enough for staff to see where they are going and leads almost directly to improvements in profitability.

Scoreboard – Month of January 2019

Lagging indicators		Target	Forecast	Gap
Susan	NSW sales	$150,000	$225,000	$75,000
Tom	VIC / TAS sales	$180,000	$90,000	-$90,000
Alex	WA sales	$100,000	$95,000	-$5,000
Phil	QLD sales	$50,000	$75,000	$25,000
Calculation	Total Revenue	$200,000	$300,000	$100,000
Alex	Total Cost of Sales	$400,000	$425,000	-$25,000
Calculation	Gross Margin	-$200,000	-$125,000	-$75,000
Owen	Overhead Expenses	$250,000	$225,000	$25,000
Calculation	Profit Before Taxes (PBT)	-$450,000	-$350,000	$100,000

Leading indicators		Target	Forecast	Gap
Maureen	NSW - referral partner meetings	0	35	35
Linda	VIC / TAS - referral partner meetings	40	25	-15
Cyndy	WA - referral partner meetings	40	10	-30
James	QLD - referral partner meetings	40	50	10
Susan	NSW - on-time performance	95%	78%	-17%
Tom	VIC/ TAS - on-time performance	95%	65%	-30%
Alex	WA - on-time performance	95%	90%	-5%
Phil	QLD - on-time performance	95%	98%	3%
Susan	NSW - net promoter score	20	17	-3
Tom	VIC / TAS - net promoter score	20	25	5
Alex	WA - net promoter score	20	20	0
Phil	Qld - net promoter score	20	19	-1

This simple scoreboard clearly shows performance against the business's key indicators – in this case, existing and new client sale percentages, revenue and total cost of sales.

Employee Participation

• While the eligibility criteria can be tailored to meet the needs of individual businesses, it is usual to require employees to have served a minimum period of employment before being invited to participate in a PPT, and to remain with the company for a specified period of time before they are able to extract the maximum benefit from participation.

- Generally, the minimum period of service will be twelve months, however you may wish to alter or waive this condition for certain staff. For example, an employee whose performance has been less than optimal may be placed on a further probationary period, while you may wish to lessen or waive the twelve-month minimum in order to attract or retain a particularly high-performing member of staff.
- In the event of an amicable resignation, the board of directors may choose to make a pro rata bonus payment to an employee. However, any amount to be paid cannot be distributed until the annual financial performance calculations are completed.
- In the event of a staff member being dismissed, no bonus should be paid for that financial year to date. It is important that this aspect be properly covered in documentation about the PPT, as well as in terms and conditions of employment, in order to ensure that employees do not have a claim against the company for withheld bonuses.
- When employees (with the consent of the company) take a period of absence, their PPT account will be frozen and funds made available in accordance with the vesting conditions on their return.

Distribution of Earnings

Participating employees are allocated units in the PPT (based on the unit allocation formula on the following page) and will earn a proportion of income and capital gains based on the number of units they hold.

Issue of Employee Units

Participation in the PPT is by invitation only at Directors' discretion. Participating employees are allocated units in the PPT based on the contributions directly made by, or apportioned to, each person. The proportion of bonus allocated to individuals is determined using a points system, which can be calculated in any number of ways.

The number of Employee Units issued to an invitee will be determined by the Trustee with reference to the following factors:

- Length of Service (pro rata for permanent part time) (25%) and excludes any breaks in employment (i.e. leave without pay) but includes all paid leave periods in accordance with standard leave entitlements;
- Role/responsibility (50%) – reflected by consideration of current role, with key metric including current base salary level (FTE); and
- Performance (25 %).

For example, an employee might be allocated one point for every $1000 in earnings (including incentives) and one additional point for each year of service. This method of points' allocation takes into consideration seniority (based on salary) and loyalty to the company (based on length of service). But there are many other ways that points can be calculated, depending on the needs of the organisation.

In the future, there may be the opportunity for staff to purchase additional Units in the PPT using their own funds. Provision of this option will be at the discretion of the company's Shareholders and Directors.

There are many other ways that units can be calculated, depending on the needs of the organisation. For some clients we have created allocation methodologies based solely on salary. For others we have created allocations based on multiple considerations, one client uses three measures: overall business profitability, team sales and individual sales. What this does is reward individual, intra-team and inter-team performance. An approach such as this sends a very clear signal to employees about the types of behaviours and results that are expected and valued by the organisation, and it drives a very cooperative and well-integrated culture in which everyone works together for mutual benefit.

Redemption of Units

The Trustee is required to sell units upon certain events including when an Employee Unit Holder is no longer eligible to stay in the PPT or when Employee Unit Holders request their Units to be sold.

When this occurs, you will be entitled to an Employee Redemption Amount. Employee Redemption Amount means the cash value of the Shares allocated to the remaining Units sold, after the application of the Disqualifying Discount, net of any costs in relation to the selling of those Allocated Shares.

You will be paid the Employee Redemption Amount as soon as practicable following the redemption of your remaining Employee Units. This is estimated to be within 6 months but will not exceed 12 months.

The most recent previous company valuation will be used for the purpose of calculating the value of the PPT.

A Disqualifying Discount applies to Employee Units issued within the company PPT for the purpose of rewarding longer term/longevity of service. The Disqualifying Discount is calculated by reference to how long an Employee Unit is held by the Employee.

Held individual Units for	Entitlement Percentage
1 Year	10%
2 Years	20%
3 Years	30%
4 Years	40%
5 Years	50%
6 Years	60%
7 Years	70%
8 Years	80%
9 Years	90%
10 Years or more	100%

Each year, the Disqualifying Discount will decrease by 10%, until year 10, when they will be able to receive 100% of the value of Units held. For example, if an Employee was to leave the PPT in the fourth year after the registration of their Units, then they would be entitled to 40% of the value of their units upon redemption.

The Disqualifying Discount will not apply:

- Where the Employee Unit Holder's employment with the Applicant is terminated due to retirement or due to extenuating circumstances as determined and agreed by the majority Shareholders of the company.
- To the proportion of Units purchased by the Employee with their own funds, including reinvestment of their share of any dividends.

For example, if an employee had held his Units for 6 years and holds shares worth $10,000, then his redemption amount would be $10,000 x 60% = $6000.

Disqualifying Events

An Employee Unit Holder's Units will be forfeited if they are the subject of a disqualifying event. Disqualifying Events are outlined in the Trust Deed as unfavourable circumstances where it would be inappropriate to redeem the full value amount of the Units. A Disqualifying Events clause ultimately protects both company and each employee participating in the PPT by discouraging behaviour that is inconsistent with the PPT's intentions and the efforts of Employee Unit Holders.

Some examples include:

- If, in the reasonable opinion of the Employer, the holder of the Employee Unit commits any fraud, dishonesty, defalcation or gross, wilful or serious misconduct in relation to the Employer.
- The holder of the Employee Unit is dismissed from employment by the Employer. For clarity, dismissal does not include retirement, redundancy or genuine resignation.
- Where it is discovered that the Employee Unit Holder has moved to a competitor while they are still employed by the company. To avoid any doubt, this does not prevent existing employees from moving to a competitor once their units have been redeemed.

Where it is discovered that the Employee Unit Holder has been charged with an indictable criminal offence punishable by a goal term which brings material disrepute or causes the company financial duress.

Additional Investments

In addition to the company-funded contributions to the trust, employees can also make additional individual investments into the PPT. Because the PPT is designed to earn income on its assets, any investments into the trust are considered to be capital, and are therefore not taxable in the hands of the trustee.

Investment Loans

Employees can borrow from the PPT in order to acquire additional equity in it. Any additional contributions made on behalf of employees who borrow from the PPT (such as bonus payments or salary sacrifice) can be used to repay the loan. One of the most common uses for investment loans from a PPT is to enable employees to fund succession. Refer to page 35 for a more detailed explanation of how this works.

Valuation

Valuation will depend on the type of investment. External investments will be based on the actual market value of the investment on the date of acquisition or disposal. Internal investments (which are usually shares in the underlying company), are nearly always valued on the basis of a multiple of earnings, which is the simplest, fairest and easiest way to determine the value of shares or equity in a private company. Publicly listed companies have a price to earnings (PE) ratio, and the same methodology applies to small businesses, but is referred to as an earnings multiple. A calculation of the value of the company shares based on an earnings multiple calculation is undertaken prior to the commencement of the PPT, and the same method is used to update the valuation.

What are the taxation implications of PPTs?

The tax implications for both employers and employees should be carefully weighed to ensure that the needs of both are considered. As with all taxation issues, this is a complex area, and you should seek individual expert advice. The taxation treatment which applies to the PPT trust, the employer, and individual employees are detailed in 3 private binding rulings which have been issued by the Australian Taxation Office.

- Trust – ATO Ruling Authorisation Number: 1051338012860
- Employer – ATO Ruling Authorisation Number: 1051314640866
- Employees – ATO Ruling Authorisation Number: 1051323914120

A PPT proves to be particularly tax advantageous when it is used for the purpose of funding internal investment into the company, or succession planning, as it becomes Fringe Benefits Tax exempt.

As mentioned in Part 1, the Government announced further proposed measures in November 2018 to simplify the employee share scheme, increase the value limit of eligible financial products available to employees to $10,000 and introduce the ability for employees to purchase additional products, if they wish.

Taxation Implications for Start-up ESOPs

Summary of Key Changes to Legislation

The Government introduced changes to the tax treatment of employee share schemes (ESS) on 1 July 2015. These changes apply to ESS interests (shares, stapled securities and rights to acquire them) issued on or after that date. The main changes announced in 2015 were to:

- to the timing of the deferred taxing point for ESS interests acquired under tax-deferred schemes, including increasing the maximum deferral to 15 years
- test for significant ownership and voting rights limitations have been eased
- that a tax refund is possible in some circumstances where an employee acquires rights but chooses not to exercise them.

Each of these are briefly discussed on the succeeding pages.

Deferred taxing point
The taxing point in tax-deferred schemes has become the earlier of:
- when there is no risk of forfeiting the ESS interests and any restrictions on their sale are lifted
- in the case of rights, when the employee has exercised them and there is no risk of forfeiting the resulting share and no restriction on disposing of that share
- when the employee ceases the relevant employment
- 15 years after the ESS interests were acquired.

Significant ownership test
The significant ownership and voting rights test has changed. All interests in the company, including rights to acquire shares, are taken into account (previously only share ownership was considered). However, an employee can acquire up to 10% ownership in the company or control up to 10% of the voting rights before their holding is considered significant and makes them ineligible for concessional treatment.

Tax refund
A refund of tax paid at the taxing point is possible if an employee acquires rights and later chooses not to exercise them or allows them to be cancelled. However, as before, a refund is not available if the employee share scheme is structured to directly protect the employee from a fall in the market value of the shares.

Concessions for start-up companies
The discount provided for eligible ESS interests will not be taxed under the ESS regime, as long as the eligibility criteria are met.

Any gain or loss on disposal of the rights or shares will be assessed under the capital gains tax regime. When working out if the 50% CGT discount applies, the period of ownership of a share acquired on exercise of a right is taken to have started when the right was acquired.

Eligibility criteria for start-up concessions

In addition to the general conditions that apply to all concessional schemes, the following specific conditions apply to the start-up concession:

- Start-up company
    - Must not be listed on any stock exchange
    - All companies in the corporate group must have been incorporated for less than 10 years
    - Aggregated annual turnover must not exceed $50 million.
- Employer
    - The employing company must be an Australian resident company.
- Scheme
    - Employees must hold ESS Interests for at least three years.
- ESS interests
    - A share must be provided at a discount no greater than 15% of the market value.
    - A right must have an exercise price (or strike price) that is greater than or equal to the market value of an ordinary share in the issuing company.

Assistance for start-up companies

There are approved market valuations methods start-up companies can use to value their unlisted shares.

We have developed a set of standard documents to help start-up companies establish an ESS, including a performance based rights plan and a standard letter for offering employees an ESS interest in the company.

Taxation Implications for the Employer

According to the Income Tax Assessment Act 1997 (ITAA), the PPT is an Employee Share Scheme as defined by Section 83A and sub-section 995-1(1) of ITAA which has been designed by Succession Plus for its clients, who are predominantly mid-market professional services businesses, to attract, retain and motivate key employees.

Deductibility

Contributions paid by the Employer to the Trust pursuant to the Peak Performance Trust Deed will be deductible in accordance with section 8-1 of the Income Tax Assessment Act 1997 (ITAA 1997).

An employer is entitled to a deduction under section 8-1 for a contribution paid to the trustee of a Trust that is either incurred in gaining or producing the Employer's assessable income, or necessarily incurred in carrying on a business for the purpose of gaining or producing the Employer's assessable income ('positive limbs').

However, subsection 8-1(2) prevents such a deduction to the extent that it is a loss or outgoing of capital, or of a capital nature, is a loss or outgoing of a private or a domestic nature, is incurred in gaining or producing exempt income or non-assessable non-exempt income or is prevented from being deductible under a specific provision of the ITAA 1997 or the ITAA 1936 ('negative limbs').

To qualify for a deduction under section 8-1, a loss or outgoing must be incurred.

Although the term 'incurred' is not defined in the legislation, reference can be made to Taxation Ruling TR 97/7 Income tax: section 8-1 – meaning of 'incurred' – timing of deductions (TR 97/7) and Taxation Ruling TR 94/26 Income tax: subsection 51(1) – meaning of incurred – implications of the High Court decision in Coles Myer Finance (TR 94/26).

Broadly, a taxpayer incurs an outgoing at the time the taxpayer owes a present money debt that they cannot escape. Otherwise a loss or outgoing is incurred when a taxpayer is definitively committed to the loss or outgoing (refer to FC of T v James Flood Pty Ltd (1953) 88 CLR

492). It is important to establish that the contributions are irretrievable and not refundable, as they will otherwise not be a permanent loss or outgoing incurred.

Timing of Deductions

Contributions paid by the Employer to the PPT according to the Trust Deed will be deductible in the income year in which the Shares acquired from the contribution are allocated to a Participant.

The provision of money to the Trustee of the Trust by the Employer for the purpose of remunerating its employees under the PPT is an outgoing in carrying on the Employer's business and is deductible under section 8-1 of the ITAA 1997.

The deduction under section 8-1 of the ITAA 1997 would generally be allowable in the income year in which the Employer incurred the outgoing but under certain circumstances, the timing of the deduction is specifically determined under section 83A-210 of the ITAA 1997.

Section 83A-210 of the ITAA 1997 provides that if:

(a) at a particular time, you provide another entity with money or other property:
    (i) under an arrangement; and
    (ii) for the purpose of enabling an individual (the ultimate beneficiary) to acquire, directly or indirectly, an ESS interest under an employee share scheme in relation to the ultimate beneficiary's employment (including past or prospective employment); and
(b) that particular time occurs before the time (the acquisition time) the ultimate beneficiary acquires the ESS interest;

then, for the purpose of determining the income year (if any) in which you can deduct an amount in respect of the provision of the money or other property, you are taken to have provided the money or other property at the acquisition time.

Section 83A-210 of the ITAA 1997 will only apply if there is a relevant connection between the money provided to the Trustee, and the acquisition of ESS interests (directly or indirectly) by the Employer under the relevant PPT in relation to the employee's employment. An ESS interest in a company is defined in subsection 83A-10(1) of the ITAA 1997 as either a beneficial interest in a share in the company or a beneficial interest in a right to acquire a beneficial interest in a share in the company.

Under the PPT, the beneficial interest in a Share granted to an employee will be an ESS interest. This ESS interest will also be granted under an employee share scheme in relation to the employee's employment.

Consequently, the provision of money to the Trustee to acquire shares in the Employer is considered to be for the purpose of enabling the participating employees, to acquire the beneficial interest in Shares. If that money is provided before the Shares are allocated to a Participant then section 83A-210 of the ITAA 1997 will apply to deny the deduction until the income year in which the beneficial interest in the Share is allocated to the Participant.

Fringe Benefits Tax

Contributions paid by the employer to the PPT does not constitute a 'fringe benefit' as defined in subsection 136(1) of the Fringe Benefits Tax Assessment Act 1986 (FBTAA).The Trust is an employee share trust, as defined in subsection 995-1(1) of the ITAA 1997, as the activities of the Trust in acquiring and allocating ESS interests meet the requirements of paragraphs 130-85(4)(a) and 130-85(4)(b) of the ITAA 1997 and its other activities are merely incidental to those activities in accordance with paragraph 130-85(4)(c) of the ITAA 1997. As such, paragraph (ha) of the definition of fringe benefit in subsection 136(1) of the FBTAA excludes the contributions to the Trustee of the Trust from being a fringe benefit. Therefore, the Employer will not be required to pay fringe benefits tax in respect of the irretrievable cash contributions it makes to the Trustee of the Trust to fund the acquisition of shares.

Anti-avoidance Part IV A

The general anti-avoidance provisions under Part IVA of the Income Tax Assessment Act 1936 (ITAA 1936) do not apply to the scheme described.

The Commissioner will not seek to make a determination that Part IVA of the ITAA 1936 applies to deny, in part or full, any deduction claimed by the Employer for contributions to the Trustee to fund the subscription for or acquisition of shares in the Employer by the Trustee. For further information, employers should refer to the ATO Ruling 1051314640866.

Taxation Implications for the Employee

Does Division 83A apply?

Division 83A of the ITAA 1997 applies to the acquisition of units by the employee from the trustee of the PPT except where the employee acquires additional units for market value consideration.

Division 83A of the ITAA 1997 applies to an employee share scheme (ESS) interest if you acquire the interest under an ESS at a discount.

Section 83A-1 states that your assessable income includes discounts on shares, rights and stapled securities you (or your associate) acquire under an employee share scheme.

Section 83A-10 states that an ESS interest, in a company, is a beneficial interest in: a share in the company; or a right to acquire a beneficial interest in a share in the company. An employee share scheme is a scheme under which ESS interests in a company are provided to employees or associates of employees, (including past or prospective employees) of the company; or subsidiaries of the company; in relation to the employees' employment.

The combined effect of section 83A-20 and paragraph 83A-105(1)(a) is that Division 83A (and in particular either Subdivision 83A-B or 83A-C) will apply to an ESS interest if you acquire the interest under an employee share scheme and at a discount.

Where you accept an invitation to acquire units in the trust for no consideration you acquires ESS interests. The combined effect of section 83A-10 and section 130-85 is that your acquisition of the units in the trust are beneficial interests in shares of the company.

Subsection 130-85(4) defines an employee share trust for an employee share scheme as a trust whose sole activities are:

(a) obtaining shares in a company; and

(b) ensuring that ESS interests in the company that are beneficial interests in those share or rights are provided under the employee share scheme to employees, or to associates of employees, of:

  (i) the company;

  (ii) or a subsidiary of the company

(c) other activities that are merely incidental to the activities mentioned in paragraphs (a) and (b).

As the Trust's sole activities are obtaining shares in the Employer and providing those shares to employees under the PPT, the trust is an employee share trust.

As you have not paid consideration for the units and the value of the units are equal to the value of the underlying shares, you are taken to have acquired the ESS interests at a discount.

The units in the Trust and therefore the ESS interests are provided to you as an incentive by your employer and as such are clearly acquired by you in relation to your employment. Therefore, Division 83A will apply to the acquisition of units by you.

However, where you acquire additional units in the trust and pay market value consideration for such units, neither of the operative Subdivisions of Division 83A will apply to the acquisition of such units. Although the interests acquired meet the definition of ESS interests in section 83A-10 and such interests are arguably acquired in relation to employment, Division 83A will only apply where such interests are acquired at a discount. Therefore, Division 83A will not apply to any additional units acquired by you at market value.

Timing of taxing point

A taxing point arises under Division 83A of the ITAA 1997 in relation to the acquisition of units by the employee in the income year in which the deferred taxing point arises for the ESS interests acquired by the employee.

Where an ESS interest is acquired under an employee share scheme in relation to the employee's employment and at a discount, section 83A-20 states that Subdivision 83A-B applies to the interest unless Subdivision 83A-C applies.

Subdivision 83A-B applies to include the discount in the year in which an ESS interest is acquired. However where the conditions in subsection 83A-105(1) are met, Subdivision 83A-C applies and the discount (i.e. the market value of the interest less its cost base) is included in the employee's assessable income in the income year in which the deferred taxing point occurs.

As the scheme is a share scheme and there is no salary sacrifice involved, the conditions which must be met for deferral to apply are those contained in subsections 83A-45(1),(2),(3) and (6) and subsections 83A-105(2) and (3).

You are a current employee of the company and so the condition in subsection 83A-45(1) is met.

Subsection 83A-45(2) applies as only beneficial interests in ordinary shares of the company will be acquired under the PPT.

Subsection 83A-45(3) applies because the company does not have a predominant business of the acquisition, holding or sale of shares.

Additional contributions by employee

Contributions made by the employee to acquire additional units in the Trust does not constitute assessable income of the employee.

When you acquire additional units at market value you are providing arms-length market value consideration for the acquisition of an asset, namely the unit. The acquisition is neither ordinary nor statutory income and the consideration provided is an outgoing and clearly not assessable.

Disqualifying event

In the event of a disqualifying event occurring in relation to employee units held by the employee section 83A-310 of the ITAA 1997 operates to treat Division 83A to be taken to never have applied to the ESS interests represented by such units.

Section 83A-310 of the ITAA 1997 provides that Division 83A (apart from Subdivision 83A-E) is taken never to have applied to an ESS interest that is a share acquired by an individual under an employee share scheme if disregarding section 83A-310 an amount is included in the individual's assessable income under Division 83A in relation to the share and the individual forfeits the share and the forfeiture is not the result of either a choice made by the individual (other than a choice to cease employment) or a condition of the scheme that has the direct effect of protecting the individual against a fall in the market value of the share.

There are no conditions in the trust deed which could be taken to have the effect of protecting the individual from a fall in the market value of the share.

The only choice that could potentially affect the individual's entitlement to the shares is a choice to cease employment. As such a choice is excluded from those which would prevent the section from operating section 83A-310 will operate to treat Division 83A to be taken to never have applied to the ESS interests represented by such units in the event of a disqualify event occurring.

CGT upon redemption

The employee will not be liable for capital gains tax on any capital gain made upon the redemption of ordinary employee units, unless the redemption of ordinary units occurs after the deferred taxing point for the ESS interest.

Subdivision 130-D of the ITAA 1997 operates to recognise that Division 83A contains the primary rules for taxing gains on ESS interests acquired under employee share schemes and that capital gains and capital losses on such interests should usually be disregarded during the period in which Division 83A applies to them.

In particular section 130-80 operates to disregard any capital gain or capital loss to the extent it results from a CGT event (other than where the capital gain or loss results from CGT events E4, G1 or K8) if the CGT event happens in relation to an ESS interest you acquire under an employee share scheme and: if Subdivision 83A-C applies to the interest the time of the acquisition is the time when the CGT event happens; or the CGT event happens on or before the ESS deferred taxing point for the interest.

As Subdivision 83A-C applies to the acquisition of ordinary units the effect of subsection 130-80 is to disregard the capital gain or capital loss from CGT events that happen from the time of acquisition up until the deferred taxing point.

Once a deferred taxing point arises in respect of the unit section 83A-125 operates inter alia to reset the cost base of the unit at its market value unless the deferred taxing point occurs at the time the unit is disposed of.

CGT upon additional acquisition

Where the employee has paid market value for the acquisition of additional employee units he will be liable for capital gains tax on any capital gain made upon the redemption of employee units?

As noted above, section 130-80 of the ITAA 1997 only operates to disregard capital gains and capital losses where either Subdivision 83A-B or Subdivision 83A-C applies to the ESS interest.

Where a unit is acquired for market value (i.e. not at a discount), neither Subdivision 83A-B or 83A-C will apply. Consequently, the acquisition of the units (and underlying shares) will constitute an acquisition of a CGT asset to which section 109-5 of the ITAA 1997 and the remainder of Part 3-1 and Part 3-3 will apply.

Anti-avoidance Part IVA

The general anti-avoidance provisions under Part IVA of the ITAA 1936 do not apply to the scheme described.

A consideration of all the factors referred to in subsection 177D(2) of the ITAA 1936 leads to the conclusion that the dominant purpose of the scheme is to provide remuneration to you in a form that promotes the Employer's business objectives, rather than to obtain a tax benefit.

Accordingly, the Commissioner will not make a determination that Part IVA of the ITAA 1936 applies to deny, in part or full, any tax benefit derived by you a result of your participation in the PPT as described.

Employees can refer to ATO Ruling 1051323914120 for further information.

Taxation implications for the Trustee

Contributions to the Trust

Amounts contributed to the trustee by employees for the acquisition of additional employee units do not constitute assessable income of the PPT. These amounts are capital and not assessable income.

Contributions of monies by employees subscribing for additional units in the trust to the trustee pursuant to the trust deed represent corpus of the trust. The contributions constitute capital receipts to the trustee and are not included in the calculation of the net income of the trust estate under section 95 of the ITAA 1936.

Employee Contribution to the Trust

Amounts contributed by the employer to the PPT for the benefit of employees do not constitute assessable income of the Trust. These amounts are capital and not assessable income.

Contributions of monies by the employer to the trustee according to the trust deed represent corpus of the trust. The contributions constitute capital receipts to the trustee, and are not included in the calculation of the net income of the trust estate under section 95 of the ITAA 1936.

Anti-avoidance – Part IVA

The general anti-avoidance provisions under Part IVA of ITAA 1936 do not apply to the scheme described. Provided that the scheme is implemented as described in this ruling, the Commissioner will not seek to make a determination that Part IVA of the ITAA 1936 applies to deny, in part or full, any tax benefit derived by the trustee as a result of his participation in the PPT as described.

A consideration of all the factors referred to in subsection 177D(2) of the ITAA 1936 leads to the conclusion that the dominant purpose of the scheme is to provide remuneration to participants in a form that promotes the Employer's business objectives, rather than to obtain a tax benefit.

Accordingly, the Commissioner will not make a determination that Part IVA of the ITAA 1936 applies to deny, in part or full, any tax benefit derived by any of the participants including the trustee as a result of their participation in the PPT as described.

Trustees of the PPT should refer to ATO Ruling 1051338012860 for further information.

Where to from here?

"If you treat staff as your equals,
they'll roll their sleeves up to get the job done."

John Ilhan

Once you have made the decision to implement a PPT within your company, the process is a relatively fast one; you could have your PPT up and running within as little as a month. A typical implementation timetable would include the following steps:

1. Agree proposal
2. Agreement recorded and invoice paid
3. Scoping meeting
4. Design
    4.1 Finalise key PPT criteria:
        4.1.1   Vesting conditions
        4.1.2   Qualifying conditions
        4.1.3   Profit benchmarks
        4.1.4   Trustee board membership
5. Documentation
    5.1 Instruct documentation
        5.1.1   PPT checklist and order form
        5.1.2   Review terms and criteria
    5.2 Documents issued
        5.2.1   Trust deed
        5.2.2   Operating manual
        5.2.3   Administration forms and templates
        5.2.4   Employee handbook
6. Education
    6.1 Staff seminar
        6.1.1   Overview to all staff
        6.1.2   Distribute and review employee handbooks
        6.1.3   Q & A session
7. Activation
    7.1 Finalise execution and implementation
8. Ongoing maintenance
    8.1 Set up PPT email for staff queries
    8.2 Provide administration form templates to client
    8.3 Review PPT product folder contents
    8.4 Schedule quarterly trustee meetings
    8.5 Schedule reporting timetable.

FAQs on
Employee Share
Ownership Plans

FAQs on ESOPs by SME Business Owners

1. **Will implementing a share plan mean I need to hand over control of my business?**

   A: NO. ESOPs are not designed to transfer control (until you are ready), they are designed to transition equity to your employees to better align your interests with theirs. In most cases we use a corporate trustee for the ESOP and the directors of the corporate trustee (which manages the ESOP) are the same as the main trading entity.

2. **Do my employees expect to pay to join?**

   A: In most cases we can design the plan so the employees can contribute, but we normally recommend this is not compulsory — otherwise you might preclude good employees who simply can't afford to write out a cheque to participate.

3. **How does this affect the normal laws regarding employment/HR?**

   A: The introduction of an ESOP does not change the employment relationship and all of the normal HR laws apply to employees who are members of an ESOP.

4. **How much equity do I need to sell-down?**

   A: There are no hard and fast rules (and no limits imposed by the taxation law governing ESOPs). We have implemented plans with as little as 10% of shares held by the ESOP and some where the ESOP is gradually buying the whole business (100 %). The amount you sell needs to be enough to be of value to employees and provide a reasonable stake in the business.

5. **When I sell, do I pay Capital Gains Tax?**

   A: YES. Your sale of shares is a taxable event for CGT, but you will still be eligible for all of the Small Business CGT concessions in the same way as if you sold the business externally.

6. How do buyers view a business with an ESOP?

A: In most cases, this is a strong advantage. In many businesses the key risk from a buyer's point of view is the risk of employees leaving immediately after a sale. While the ESOP cannot stop this, it can certainly reduce the risk by locking employees in with an equity stake. Many plans which are introduced in the lead up to sale include a stay bonus – an extra contribution made to the ESOP if for example, employees stay for 24 months after the sale. In some cases, the buyer will have an ESOP already and simply roll your employees into their plan, many will just continue the existing plan, while in some cases, the buyer may choose to pay out the plan.

FAQs on ESOPs by Employees

1. What is my risk? What if the company owes money?

A: Employees who are members of an employee share plan are protected from any of the liabilities of the employer company and would not be liable for any debts or monies owed. Nor are they required to contribute to any losses incurred by the company.

2. Can I own the shares in a family trust or my self-managed super fund?

A: In most cases the answer is NO. Unfortunately, many of the benefits are only available to employees and therefore the shares or options must also be owned by the employee in their own name.

3. Does being a member of an employee share plan affect the terms of my employment?

A: NO. The share plan rules and qualifying conditions etc., relate only to the employee share plan and does not have any effect on the laws which govern your employment including any enterprise bargaining agreement, award or other arrangement.

4. **If the share plan earns dividends from my employer, do these come to me and if so, do I pay tax on them?**

   A: YES. In all of the various structures the employee share plan would normally act as a "flow-through" device and in the case of the trust structure that is commonly used, any given or distributions we see, need to be passed through to the individual employees and paid in cash. At that point they would be taxed as part of the employees individual income at marginal tax rates. In many cases dividends would include franking credits and these also are through to the employee.

5. **What happens if I leave the company?**

   A: Except in very specific and unusual circumstances leaving employment would be disqualifying admit and in most of the plans this simply would mean that you are no longer able to the shares or options as you are no longer an employee. In many cases disqualifying events are also accompanied by disqualifying discount and so the value of your shares or options may be reduced, especially if you "leave early."

6. **Am I now a director of the company or entitled to a seat on the board?**

   A: NO. The employee share plan does not include any right to become a director of the company and in fact most employees do not want to become directors as this may well make them liable other areas. Typically, when a share plan becomes a majority owner in the company, then the sheer plan may have the right to elect an employee to join the board of directors. This though is a matter for agreement between the employees and the current directors/founders of the company.

7. **What information will I receive on the performance of the company?**

   A: Employee share clan members will always receive an annual statement which shows the number of units they hold and the underlying value of the shares in the company. The plan administrators will need to complete an annual valuation of the business as part of this process and that will always include a review of financial statements. Most employers provide a summarised version of this information to ESOP members.

8. **What happens if the company is sold?**

   A: In the event that the company is sold externally there are two possibilities:

   (a) Members of the employee share plan are "forced" to sell at the same time as the founders and would therefore be paid out the value of their shares at the time of the sale.

   (b) The buyer decides to keep the employee share plan in place and continues to make contributions etc. in the same way that the original owners did.

ACADEMIC RESEARCH ON ESOPs

Part 3 provides those business owners, financial planners, accountants and advisers extensive research, case studies and evidence about employee share ownership plans.

An employee share scheme (ESS), also referred to as an employee share option plan, employee share ownership scheme or an employee equity scheme, is a remuneration scheme under which firms offer to their employees shares, stapled securities or rights to acquire them (options). (Department of Parliamentary Services, 2015) ESS should not be confused with Cooperative, Mutual and Member-owned firms, (Senate Economics Reference Commitee, 2016) which may or may not have an ESS.

Employee Share Ownership Plans (ESOPs) are identified as a means of enhancing enterprise performance through promoting worker productivity. (Relations., 2000) There have also been studies related to use as a means of reducing agency costs through directly monitoring employees and through adopting incentive-based forms of remuneration. (Pendleton, 2006) Principal – agent behavioural theory argues that employee logical self-interest, aversion to risk and effort creates costs for an organisation. In the absence of complete information, the principal (business owner) has to increase productivity through a mixture of compensation and monitoring of agents (employees). ESOPs are a way to align principal and agents efforts to improve productivity, however, a free rider effect is expected to diminish the effect of ESOPs in larger firms. (Sesil & Lin, 2011) They have also been argued to reduce wealth inequality and improve firm and aggregate economic outcomes. (Kozlowski, 2013) ESOPs are also considered by policy makers and advocates to be an important mechanism to encourage Start-up activity by enabling Australian employers to improve cash flows and attract and retain talented staff at lower rates of wage compensation (when supplemented with shares or options) (Department of Prime Minister and Cabinet, 2014).

According to (I. Landau, Mitchell, O'Connell, & Ramsey, 2007) employee share ownership "has enjoyed bipartisan support in Australia." Obviously, ESOPs can take many different forms and use many different structures to implement what is broadly described as an Employee

Ownership model. There are two key models which vary primarily in the amount of equity they offer for employee ownership. "One category provides benefits to executives while the other is aimed at general employees" (R. Brown & Lau, 1997, p. 34) Firstly, majority employee-owned firms consist of active employee involvement, and a strong sense of ownership and employees are more involved in the corporate governance and decision-making processes. secondly, minority plans, those typically found in larger companies and offering a far smaller amount of equity for employee ownership, the plans are often a component of the companies' overall remuneration and incentive planning and employees have little interest in governance or management participation. French (1987) accordingly argues that the orientation of minority plans is primarily focused on being part of a remuneration strategy.

The use of ESOPs varies internationally, as does the numbers of employee participants. The USA is seen as the leader of employee ownership with ESOPs emerging as early as the 1920's (Blair, 2000). The most recent wave of use commenced in the mid-1970s when specific ESOP legislation was introduced. According to the National Centre for Employee Ownership in the USA 11,500 companies use an ESOP encompassing 13.5 million employees and US$213 billions of ownership capital. The total of the various ESOP structures is estimated to involve about 20% of the US private sector workforce in share ownership (J. Blasi, Kruse, D. and Bernstein, A., 2003).

In simple terms, employee ownership provides employees with additional rights to those normally expected; a right to share in the company's profits, access to information on company finances and operations, and rights to participate in management (Rousseau & Shperling, 2003). However, there are multiple types of plans and multiple parameters within those plans, the extent to which employees are entitled to profits, information, management and participation rights varies considerably (Ben-Ner & Jones, 1995). "This variety means generalisations about employee share ownership have to be made with caution." (Kaarsemaker, Pendleton, & Poutsma, 2010, p. 316) According to survey data, the main reason for Australian firms introducing employee share ownership plans is to motivate, attract and retain competitive and valuable employees (Landau, O'Connell, & Ramsey, 2013).

Legislative framework and issues

Importantly, there is no single legislative framework for employee share ownership plans – these schemes are covered by various aspects of corporations and taxation law. The Corporations Act 2001 (Cth) contains many of the general requirements concerning disclosure, fundraising and licensing that are relevant to both the initial implementation and ongoing management of the ESOP. While the legislation contains specific provisions relating to employee share schemes it does not provide for separate or different treatment of employee-owned shares. An ASIC class order does provide some conditional relief for companies that introduce complying schemes.

The most significant issues arise when dealing with smaller privately held entities – for example, the prospectus requirement may not be onerous for companies associating an ESOP as part of an initial public offering (IPO) – "they are very significant and often insurmountable for small /medium unlisted companies." (Young, 1999).

The corporate regulatory regime is commonly criticised for imposing costs and compliance costs that may effectively deny unlisted companies access to ESOPs (Australian Employee Ownership Association, 2007). The government's report (ESODU) found in 2004 that "burdensome corporations law requirements" were imposing a "significant barrier" to businesses taking up an ESOP (TNS Social Research, 2004). Company views on regulatory reform, highlight several critical concerns including the strong suggestion (64%) to introduce a single piece of legislation to clarify the multiple overlapping legislative issues, an increase in the $1000 concession (77%) and improvements to tax-deferred plans (Div. 83A).

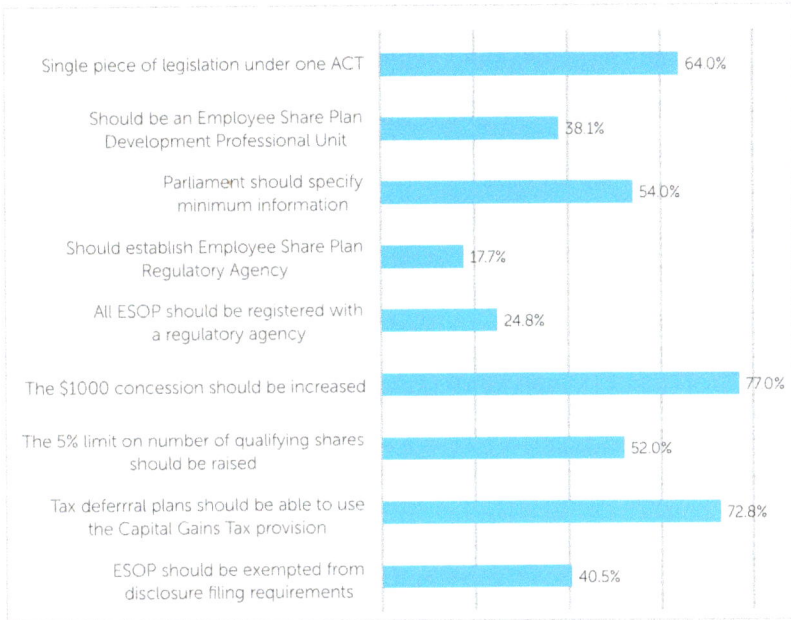

Single piece of legislation under one ACT — 64.0%
Should be an Employee Share Plan Development Professional Unit — 38.1%
Parliament should specify minimum information — 54.0%
Should establish Employee Share Plan Regulatory Agency — 17.7%
All ESOP should be registered with a regulatory agency — 24.8%
The $1000 concession should be increased — 77.0%
The 5% limit on number of qualifying shares should be raised — 52.0%
Tax deferrral plans should be able to use the Capital Gains Tax provision — 72.8%
ESOP should be exempted from disclosure filing requirements — 40.5%

(I. Landau et al., 2013, p. 73)

Taxation law and treatment

In July 2015, the Australian government introduced several changes to the legislation covering the taxation of Employee Share Plans, these changes apply to ESS interests (shares, stapled securities and rights to acquire them) issued on or after that date. There were changes to some existing rules as well as new concessions for employees of start-up companies. The main changes introduced are

- to the timing of the deferred taxing point for ESS interests acquired under tax-deferred schemes, including increasing the maximum deferral to 15 years
- the test for significant ownership and voting rights limitations have been eased so that an individual may own up to 10%
- that a tax refund is possible in some circumstances where an employee acquires rights but chooses not to exercise them.

In addition, for eligible start-up companies, where the company cannot be listed, they must have been incorporated for less than 10 years and they must have an aggregated turnover of less than $50 million, new concessions where introduced which provided for no upfront taxation on discount to market value and for any gain (or loss) to be assessed under the capital gains tax regime.

Several of the taxation concessions provided to employee share plans are dependent upon meeting several conditions, some of which are contrary to the business aims of those implementing the plan. For example, the concessions available thru the rules in Div83a are based upon the scheme being non-discriminatory – this is defined as being offered to at least 75% of employees with more than three years' service, often in an SME, employers are looking to incentivise only key/senior employees, typically far less than 75% of the employees.

The newly introduced, Div83A has in fact made the conditions for accessing the concessions more demanding and costly for SME's, Landau, O'Connell and Ramsay (I. O. C. Landau, A. Ramsay, I., 2013) state that this is mainly because whilst the government is seeking to encourage employee share ownership, it is overly concerned that the concessions may be subject to abuse. (S., 2000) Mong, in fact, argues that the rules are too strict and have restricted the growth of employee share ownership in Australia. In the dissenting report to Shared Endeavours, the minority argued that the concessions have led to plans "become vehicles for aggressive tax planning for the benefit of company executives (Rider, 2005) Further, wariness of ongoing reform has been attributed at least in part to fear by Treasury of abuse (Price, 2003).The 10% limit on shareholdings by individuals can serve to prevent SME's from accessing the taxation concessions. It also prevents employee or management buyouts from occurring under Div. 83AA (Relations, 2000).

Influence of tax incentives and disclosure relief – this graph highlights the influence taxation law and treatment has for business owners.

Note taken from (I. Landau et al., 2013, p. 72)

1. Determinants of Employee Share Ownership

In general terms, small, minority equity stakes are often acquired by employees of larger listed entities (Pendleton, 2001). The literature here is substantial and tends to focus on Agency Theory, that is, on the principal-agent framework and the issue of how the principal gets the agent to do what the principal wants (M. M. Jensen, W., 1976). Agency Theory states that optimal employee arrangements will be a tradeoff between incentives and risk. There is a substantial volume of material in the remuneration literature that higher risk facing firms are less likely to use incentive-based pay arrangements, possibly due to employee risk aversion (Bloom & Milkovich, 1998). Some additional key factors have been identified as being related to the use of ESOPs including:

A. Size

Many studies (Festing et al. 1999; Kruse 1996; Pendleton et al. 2001; Landau et al. 2007) find that size is widely associated with the adoption and use of Employee Share Ownership Plans (ESOPs). ESOPs appear to be more suitable for larger firms for various reasons most notably lower transaction costs (Lenne, Mitchell, & Ramsay, 2006). As noted above this is one of the key variables proposed to inhibit the adoption of ESOPs in Australia.According to the ESODU research, while 30% of large businesses (those with more than 100 employees), 39% of companies with more than 50 offices in Australia and 32% of companies with an annual turnover of $50 million had ESOPs only 8% of private companies had ESOPs and 9% of small businesses (5–19 employees) had ESOPs. The Shared endeavours report recognised that the adoption rate of ESOPs since its introduction in Australia in the 1970s in the unlisted sector has been significantly lower than in the listed sector (Relations., 2000, pp. 21–22).

B. Employment/workplace characteristics

The research in this space appears to be uncertain and often contradictory. There is some support that ESOPs are most prevalent in professional sectors, such as professional services and IT (Kruse, Blasi, & Park, 2007). While others suggest that ESOPs are most likely to be used when production is human capital intensive on the basis that there is a more extensive, often less skilled, workforce that is more difficult to monitor (Jones, 2006).

Other studies have not found that workforce composition is related to use of share plans (Pendleton, 2001). One study found negative relationships between share plans and teamwork on the basis of the free rider problem whereby benefits are distributed amongst a large number of employees, and therefore individual incentives become diluted (Kruse, 1996).

C. Risk

Agency theory states that optimal contracts between employees and owners will consist of a delicate balance between incentives and risk. However, a 2002 study (Prendergast, 2002) suggests a positive relationship between risk and incentives based on the theory that in more uncertain settings the principal is better off delegating responsibility and this requires the use of incentives such as ESOPs.

An additional consideration is the increased risk because of concentration – both incomes from employment and investment in the same business create a concentration of risk in one asset. If the business fails, then both income and investment are at risk, in many cases lost. A 1996 US study (Kruse, 1996) suggests that employee-owners have superior retirement provisions even excepting their ESOP stake, mainly because their firms are more likely to have defined benefit pension plans.

D. Liquidity
Firms with cash flow constraints and a high need for capital, which often can only be sourced at higher costs externally, may substitute equity compensation for cash payments to employees to reduce the cash required. While this usually is not succession related it does highlight the funding aspect (and hence perceived cost) of ESOPs (Core & Guay, 2001). An additional perspective is that share plans signal to employees that investment in human capital will be protected, the analysis reveals that an ESOP is more likely to be engaged "in a workplace that depends upon and encourages employees to make valuable investments in their human capital... the evidence confirms the influential and independent role that employee share ownership plays in supporting human capital" (Robinsons, 2005, p. 484). The lower liquidity of unlisted firms and the difficulties in determining objectively the fair market value, both at the time of take up and the employees exit, are fundamental difficulties in implementing broad-based employee share plans in unlisted firms (I. Landau et al., 2013, p. 55).

2. Employee Participation
This issue of employee participation in ESOPs, while relevant, has been disregarded mainly until recently as much of the early work was focused on majority-owned plans, and so the issue is mostly irrelevant as typically all employees received shares. Newer work focuses on the predominantly financial orientation of employees and that income, and therefore employees capacity to participate is a key influencer (Dewe, 1998).

A recent European work, based on the European working conditions survey of 2005 (Blaszczyk, 2014) found that those employees in managerial/senior positions are more than four times more likely to participate as compared to unskilled workers. Accordingly, employee interest in participation is one of the factors identified as potentially impacting on ESOP adoption in Australia. Participants in a Melbourne study (I. O. C. Landau, A. Ramsay, I,. 2013), consistently with previous remarks (Stradwick, 2000) and overseas research (Pendleton, 2002), cited employee recruitment and retention as one of the most critical goals for unlisted entities to implement ESOPs in practice. Australian ESS policy may benefit from additional incentives that encourage collective shareholding by employees (eg trusts) to limit the 'free rider' problem or incentivise complementary management practices (e.g. high level of information sharing) that encourage an innovative, cooperative culture (Conyon & Freeman, 2001; Kruse, 1996; Sesil & Lin, 2011).

3. Impact on employee attitudes and performance

There exists a large volume of academic research which is almost overwhelmingly positive in terms of the impact of an ESOP on employee attitude and performance starting as long ago as 1987 (Klein, 1987). The study identified three key aspects of employee ownership affecting attitudes and behavioral change – intrinsic satisfaction where ownership per se is sufficient to bring about attitudinal and behavioural change; extrinsic satisfaction, when ownership leads to attitudinal and behavioural change because it is financially rewarding; and instrumental satisfaction where ownership brings about change by facilitating other outcomes that are desired by employees such as more involvement and participation in decision making (Klein, 1987). This work was further developed by Brown, Pierce and Crossley (2014) who proposed that employee share ownership leads to a change in employee mindset and ultimately attitudinal and behavioural change.

Although all prior studies results have been equally positive, several gaps in the research appear. For example, the question of what level of share ownership does real attitudinal change take place has not been examined. The relationship between the level of employee share ownership and the level of performance is also strongly linked to culture and employee involvement (Beyster, 2007). Ownership alone does not necessarily lead to performance improvements, but employee involvement (Kato & Morishima, 2002) and company culture combined with ownership tend to lead to improved performance (Sengupta, Whitfield, & McNabb, 2007).

Also, several studies have focused on employee wealth and wages relating to ESOPs. For example, Blair (2000) found 8% higher compensation levels in public companies where broad-based ESOP plans held at least 5% of company stock. (Kardas, Scharf, Keogh, & Rodrick, 1998) confirmed that the levels of pay and other benefits were similar between ESOP and non-ESOP firms in companies in Washington State in the US and proposed that this was an indicator of the fact that ownership wealth from ESOPs does not substitute for present-day income, but instead comes in addition to worker pay and benefits and thus results in far greater overall compensation packages in ESOP companies, and potentially more significant employee loyalty and engagement.

Regarding employment stability Blair (2000) also found substantial evidence of increased job stability in US public companies with broad-based employee ownership plans as compared to otherwise similar firms. ESOPs typically lead to a reduction in employee turnover which may result in increases in productivity.(Sesil & Lin, 2011) Employee turnover is also a reasonable measure of employee satisfaction and highly correlated to both firm and employee performance. (Park & Shaw, 2013).

Using a scale documented by Rosen, Klein and Young (Rosen, Klein, & Young, 1986) to test for satisfaction with ESOP participation 80.4% of respondents indicated they were "proud" to own shares in their company and 51.7% that it was "very important" to them that their company had an ESOP. Only 4.5% of shareholders "didn't care" about their company's ESOP.

4. Impact on workplace and company performance
Several studies emphasise the capacity of ESOPs to retain valuable employees either by signalling the firms commitment to their employees (Robinsons, 2005) by locking in employees through the deferred nature of share plans (Sengupta et al., 2007), or by linking employee rewards to the business cycle (Oyer, 2004). In addition, there are multiple studies (Beyster, 2007; Doucouliagos, 1995; Kaarsemaker et al., 2010; Kato &

Morishima, 2002) on the financial, productivity and profitability effects of an ESOP which are almost all positive. Most of these studies indicate that the improvements are often individually small but undoubtedly more significant when two things are combined – majority employee ownership (Doucouliagos, 1995) and employee participation and involvement in decision making (Kato & Morishima, 2002). Significantly (Sengupta et al., 2007, p. 152) concludes that "a substantial part of the explanation of this positive association with labour productivity and financial performance is due to the promotion of lower labour turnover in share ownership workplaces".

Kruse (1996) summarises the results of eleven studies evaluating the comparison of performance before and after the adoption of an ESOP, ESOP to non-ESOP firms and post-adoption performance to matched non-ESOP firms. The study concludes that on average on all the performance categories, ESOP companies do better per year than non-ESOP companies and that companies do better post-adoption than pre-adoption. They estimate the average increase in performance across tests and across studies to be 4% annually (Kruse, 1996).

In a project report sponsored by the National Centre for Employee Ownership (NCEO) (Kruse et al., 2007) examined all privately held companies with ESOPs in 1988, and found that they had a much higher survival rate than closely matched firms without ESOPs. Of the 1176 private companies with ESOPs in 1988, 69.6% survived through 1999, compared to only 54.8% of non-ESOP companies in the same industry and of the same size.

In a more detailed study in 2016, (Blasi, Freeman, & Kruse, 2016) the researchers conclude that shared capitalist forms of pay are associated with high-trust supervision, participation in decisions, and information sharing, and with a variety of positive perceptions of company culture. At the firm level, shared capitalist forms of pay are associated with lower voluntary turnover and higher ROE.

Further, Blasi (2003) analysed seventy empirical studies they could find on the effects of employee stock ownership, broad-based stock options, profit sharing, and employee participation (which they describe as the four key aspects of "partnership capitalism"). They found that adoption of any of the four forms of partnership capitalism results, on average, in the gains listed in Table 3 below.

Table 3. Investor Gains from Sharing Ownership (Blasi et al., 2003)	
Performance measure	Gain from employee ownership
Average employee ownership	8% -- after dilution
Productivity	4%
Return on equity	14%
Return on assets	12%
Profit margins	11%
Total shareholder returns	2% -- after dilution!

In other words, the studies show that on average, companies and their investors made a profit on partnership approaches, including stock options, over and above other incentives offered to employees. They gave workers an 8% ownership stake, and in return enjoyed an average of a two-percentage-point higher return, even after considering the dilution of equity after 8% of the equity was allocated to employees. Based on the ABS (2015) Economic Activity Survey Small and Medium Enterprises with an ESS had a 94% growth rate in sales and a 56% growth rate in value add per employee over a three year period, as compared to 62% and 29% respectively for SME's without an ESS. (Office of the Cheif Economist, 2017).

Seventy-five percent of 139 firms surveyed by the University of Melbourne either agreed or strongly agreed that having a broad-based ESS encouraged increased productivity (I.O.C. Landau, A. Ramsay, I., 2013).

5. Participation

It has been regularly argued that employee participation in decision making is a key contributing factor to the likelihood of ESOPs being able to secure attitudinal change and achieve improvements in company productivity, and these arguments have been accepted mainly by policymakers (Blaszczyk, 2014).

In a relatively recent study (M.M. Brown, Rowan; O'Connell, Ann; Ramsay, Ian, 2012) reports the results of a survey of a group of employees who were asked to rank several factors as the essential elements of an ESOP. The study found the following factors as ranked by percentage of employees who found them to be significant:

- Financial payoff (68%)
- Fair treatment (67%)
- A sense of community (59%)
- Employee influence on management of the Company (42%)
- Individual influence on decisions affecting daily work (38%).

While the first factor is financial and relatively obvious, the other factors are not related to financial issues and are more focused on employee involvement, engagement and influence, and indicate that while financial pay-off was the most significant issue, the combination of other issues would seem more important to most employees.

Additional research amongst companies who did have an ESOP in place, strongly supports the focus on alignment of interests, shared financial success and attracting and retaining key employees. This graph from the study (I. Landau et al., 2013, p. 159) shows the very high percentage of employers looking to attract and retain key employees as well as aligning staff interests and sharing financial success as well as a mechanism to show the company values its employees. It is clear the predominant objectives are based on workplace relations or human resource management rationales.

SUCCESSION+

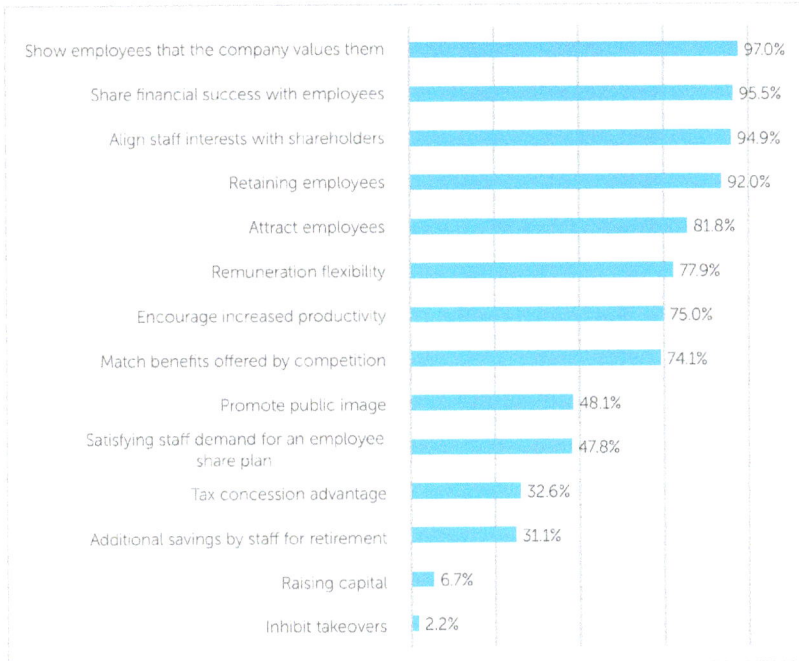

Show employees that the company values them	97.0%
Share financial success with employees	95.5%
Align staff interests with shareholders	94.9%
Retaining employees	92.0%
Attract employees	81.8%
Remuneration flexibility	77.9%
Encourage increased productivity	75.0%
Match benefits offered by competition	74.1%
Promote public image	48.1%
Satisfying staff demand for an employee share plan	47.8%
Tax concession advantage	32.6%
Additional savings by staff for retirement	31.1%
Raising capital	6.7%
Inhibit takeovers	2.2%

In the same study, (I. Landau et al., 2013, p. 161) a detailed list of potential barriers where identified by companies who did not have an ESOP, shows a broad and diverse list of potential barriers with no individual item achieving higher than 40% - "this may suggest that many respondents have simply not considered ever having an ESOP or were apathetic towards the practice" (I. Landau et al., 2013, p. 162). In comparison with the ESODU research (Department of Employment and Workplace Relations, 2004) which asked a similar question and reported four main barriers: a perception of lack of relevance of employee share ownership to the business, practical issues regarding tax and legal complexities, employee resistance and expensive set-up and maintenance costs, the results are remarkably similar.

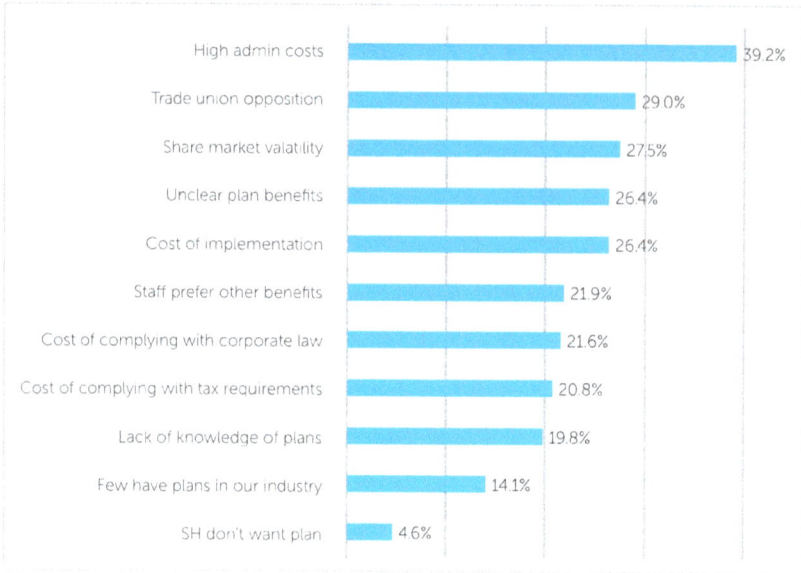

High admin costs	39.2%
Trade union opposition	29.0%
Share market valatility	27.5%
Unclear plan benefits	26.4%
Cost of implementation	26.4%
Staff prefer other benefits	21.9%
Cost of complying with corporate law	21.6%
Cost of complying with tax requirements	20.8%
Lack of knowledge of plans	19.8%
Few have plans in our industry	14.1%
SH don't want plan	4.6%

International comparison

"The incidence of ESOPs in Australian firms is growing but appears low relative to European and US firms." (Office of the Cheif Economist, 2017, p. 14) The depth and breadth of employee share ownership appear to be higher in the United Kingdom than in Australia. In 2000, 23% of UK workplaces surveyed had some form of ESOP. (Gill & Krieger, 2000) based on Australian Tax Office records the numbers of employees receiving ESS payments increased from 227,000 in 2009–10 to 335,000 in 2013–14, this represents 2.91% of the labour force (Statistics, 2016).

Glossary

Balance sheet
A detailed statement summarising the assets and liabilities of a business and giving a picture of its wealth at a particular time.

Capital
The accounting concept of capital refers to issued capital and retained earnings of the company, representing the owners' or shareholders' initial contribution to the business and the wealth that generates.

Capital gain
The result of selling a capital asset at a higher price than it cost. Whether an investor makes a capital gain or not depends on the purchase price of an asset compared to its selling price, the effect of depreciation on its value and whether inflation has bitten into the investor's profit margin.

Capital gains tax
A tax on income (gain) arising from changes in the market value of assets.

Company tax
A tax levied on the income of companies, separately from the income of its shareholders.

Deferred dividend shares
Shares issued with the stipulation that shareholders will only be entitled to receive dividends after a specified period, either because the issuing company is incurring losses or because it wants to use the funds for other purposes.

Dividend
What is paid out of a company's profits to its shareholders, usually yearly (final dividend) and sometimes half-yearly (interim dividend).

Dividend reinvestment plan

A scheme enabling shareholders in a company to acquire additional shares instead of taking their dividends in cash. For companies, the plans represent a relatively inexpensive source of equity finance. Once a shareholding is registered with a plan, reinvestment takes place automatically each time the company declares a dividend and the shareholder receives a new share certificate.

Dividend yield

The theoretical return on an investment, assuming shares are bought on the market at the prevailing price and not taking into account charges such as brokerage. It is calculated by dividing the dividend per share by the current share price, expressed as a percentage.

Earnings per share

One of a number of gauges of a company's performance. It is calculated by dividing the company's earnings by the number of shares on issue to show the profit earned in terms of each share.

Employee share ownership plan

One of a variety of incentive schemes, usually for the benefit of senior executives, through which a company rewards prized employees by giving them part-ownership. This may come in the form of shares paid for by the company, partly-paid or contributing shares made available to the employee for a minimal outlay, or options to acquire shares at a later time. Sometimes the transfer of shares will be dependent on the employee's promise to stay with the company for a specified time, or on the achievement of a performance target. Where shares are financed by loans from the company, the shares may be held in a trust, with dividends being used to pay off the loans.

Equity

The part of something – asset, house or company – which you own. What the professionals call shares. If you lend a company money, you have made a loan and rank as a creditor who, under normal circumstances, would expect repayment of the loan plus interest at a future date. If you buy ordinary shares in a company you become an equity-holder in that company, which means you share in its profits (and losses) and have a less clear-cut idea of your future returns than does a lender. As an ordinary shareholder, you stand in line behind debenture-holders for settlement, should the company be wound up. You cannot rely on a fixed return, and you run the risk of loss, but in return for this you have a share in the company's surplus during good times.

Equity trust
A unit trust which gathers unitholders' funds and invests them in a range of shares through the stockmarket.

Financial incentive
An offer of money, to induce an improvement in performance.

Fringe benefits tax
Taxes paid by employers on the value of fringe benefits provided to employees.

Fully paid shares
Shares on which no uncalled capital is due.

Golden handcuffs
Handsome remuneration made on the provision that the employee will stay with the company.

Golden hello
A generous upfront payment made by a company to an incoming employee. Similar to a signing-on fee.

Goods and services tax
An indirect tax, levied as a percentage added to the prices charged for most goods and services.

Incentive

A reward; employers offer incentives to cultivate loyalty and productivity among workers.

Income tax

Tax levied directly on personal income.

Management buy-out

A transfer of ownership or control of a company to those who are involved in running the business.

Leveraged buy-out

A method of buying a company using borrowed money, generally undertaken by the company's existing management.

Listed company

A company whose shares are quoted on the stock exchange and are available to be bought and sold by the general public.

Market capitalisation

The stockmarket's assessment of a company's value, calculated by multiplying the number of shares on issue by the current share price.

Net profit

Gross profit less all expenses such as cost of goods sold, selling expenses, tax and interest on borrowings.

Operating profit/loss

The after-tax profit or loss made by a business from its ordinary revenue-producing activities. Gains and losses derived from activities outside the normal operations of a business are called 'extraordinary items' and are added to or deducted from operating profit to arrive at a 'net profit/loss after extraordinaries'.

Option

A contract which gives the holder, in return for paying a premium to the option seller, the right to buy or sell a financial instrument or commodity during a given period.

Option stocks

Company shares on which options are traded. The Australian Stock Exchange allows option trading on only a limited range of shares.

Ordinary shares

Fully paid shares which carry voting rights but rank after debentures and preference shares for dividend payments. If the company is wound up, ordinary shareholders rank as unsecured creditors, behind secured creditors such as debenture holders.

Profit-and-loss account

An account showing a company's earnings and expenses over a period, what it has done with its profits, how much is being paid out in dividends and how much is retained in the company.

Redeemable preference shares

Shares which, on a stated maturity date, the issuing company will buy back for face value plus dividend. Being preference shares, they rank ahead of ordinary shares, but behind debentures, in any claim on the assets of the company.

Revenue

Earnings; what a company makes in monetary terms from its activities. Not to be confused with profit, since expenses have to come out of revenue.

Shareholders' funds

What belongs to the shareholders of a company: issued capital and retained profits.

Shareholders' interest

The net amount of a company's funds that belongs to its shareholders. The shareholders' ratio is calculated by dividing shareholders' funds by total assets of the company.

Unit trust

An investment product which enables small investors to pool their funds and earn a greater return than if each investor had acted individually. The investors hold units which may fluctuate in value depending on the market performance of the underlying assets. Definitions based on information from The Language of Money by Edna Carew, a dictionary of financial terms available as an online resource at www.anz.com.

Build It
Craig West

Ask any owner of a small or medium-sized business what their greatest challenge yet most valuable asset is, and they'll all agree – it's their staff. What would it mean to your business if your employees were as committed to achieving success as you are?

With more than 20 years' experience as a strategic accountant and adviser to small businesses, Craig West introduces the Peak Performance Trust – the ultimate employee engagement tool that will have your high-performing staff thinking and acting less like employees and more like business owners.

The ability to motivate people to peak performance means being able to attract and retain business – and it is a major source of competitive advantage. Can your business afford to not have a Peak Performance Trust?

For more worksheets, articles, advice and information on employee incentive schemes visit www.successionplus.com.au.